Thank You for Firing Me!

How to Catch the Next Wave of Success After You Lose Your Job

Kitty Martini and Candice Reed

STERLING and the distinctive Sterling logo are registered trademarks of Sterling Publishing Co., Inc.

Library of Congress Cataloging-in-Publication Data

Martini, Kitty.
Thank you for firing me! : how to catch the next wave of success after you lose your job / Kitty Martini & Candice Reed.
p. cm.
ISBN 978-1-4027-6956-6
1. Career changes. 2. Job hunting. 3. Vocational guidance. I. Reed, Candice. II. Title.
HF5384.M37 2010
650.14--dc22

2009034298

10 9 8 7 6 5 4 3 2 1

Published by Sterling Publishing Co., Inc.
387 Park Avenue South, New York, NY 10016
© 2010 by Kitty Martini and Candice Reed
Distributed in Canada by Sterling Publishing
C/o Canadian Manda Group, 165 Dufferin Street
Toronto, Ontario, Canada M6K 3H6
Distributed in the United Kingdom by GMC Distribution Services
Castle Place, 166 High Street, Lewes, East Sussex, England BN7 1XU
Distributed in Australia by Capricorn Link (Australia) Pty. Ltd.
P.O. Box 704, Windsor, NSW 2756, Australia

Sterling ISBN 978-1-4027-6956-6

For information about custom editions, special sales, premium and corporate purchases, please contact Sterling Special Sales Department at 800-805-5489 or specialsales@sterlingpublishing.com.

Contents

Acknowledgments

A warm and fuzzy thank you to our agent, Sammie Justesen, who saw the possibilities in our idea and how this book could make a difference for millions of people who have lost their livelihoods as well as their sense of humor. Special thanks to Meredith Hale, Tricia Medved, Kate Zimmerman, and Scott Amerman, our editors at Sterling, for bringing this book to life. A big shout-out to our first copyeditor, Maria Foster Kirkpatrick, for her sharp eye and observations. Thanks to Ralph T. Reed for getting us through our first three chapters—sorry about all the martinis you had to consume. Heartfelt kudos to Crista McClure-Swan and *At Home Magazine* for being the catalyst that brought us together. Thank you so much to Kim Rahilly who gave us some of our greatest resources. The following smart people, writers, journalists, and editors offered their knowledge and time, and we sincerely thank you: Valerie Fanning, Ciaran Clayton, Ken McCabe, Edwina Villegas, Tina Reed, Linda Tieman, Karen Drew, William T. Reed, Kehau Cerizo, Lindsey Mead McCrea, John Lang, and of course, Mark Walker. And lastly, to everyone who has hired and fired us over the years, teaching us that we were not meant to be truck drivers/funeral directors/go-go-dancers/weight loss counselors/birthday party clowns or any of the other short-lived positions we have held, and instead made us realize that we were meant to be anticareer experts! Thank You for Firing Us!

Kitty Martini

I'd like to send a million thanks to Lisa M., who fired me from my copy-writing job. If you hadn't fired me, I wouldn't have had an idea and an opportunity to help the thousands of people who have lost their jobs when the economy tanked. And wow, being unemployed sure gave me plenty of time to write this book! A big fat *mucho gracias* and *merci beau-coup* goes to my friend and coauthor, Candice Reed, whose hilarious wit, talent, and her commando ADD skills helped this book materialize. I'm ever so thankful to my funny and fabulous Italian mom, Ginny "the Shark" Aradio, who gave me daily shots of "go for it, Kid!" and magically turned my lemons into lemon drop martinis. Thank you Alexa and Kristof, my awesome kids, who ran the house while Mom was writing, and Thierry for your support, encouragement, and keeping those kids out of my hair. A happy, fluffy boatload of heartfelt appreciation goes to Darla, Daria, and Rick, my supercool siblings, who taught me that stupid jokes and writing could be a career option. Kudos to my "besties" who cheered from the sidelines: Malibu Mike, Eddie G., Windy, and Jonathan. And lastly, a million more thanks to John "Johnny D" Del Gaizo for being my muse and sparkplug for every idea that spews out of my brain and lands on stage or in a book.

Candice Reed

Without Kitty and her unique attitude and approach to life this book may never have been born. Her dry wit and crazy stories are greatly appreciated and well suited to a writer such as myself. Thank you for bringing me along for the ride my friend.

I am indebted to my talented partners in the writing community who empathize with me when I piss and moan about this thing called writing—Ruth Marvin Webster and Heather Anderson. Thanks for being there when I need you. Much appreciation to all of my former newspaper and magazine editors, but especially to Maria Foster for teaching me how to be a real journalist—I will try to remember the proper usage of an apostrophe.

For all my friends and relatives who were surprised that I became a writer but are proud of me now that I'm going to be semifamous— Craig and Carolee Engstrand, the Boneys, the Olsons, and all of those Reeds—a million thanks for listening to my stories and putting up with me over the years.

To Cathy Agrella, my friend and angel—you were my inspiration as I wrote the pages on reinventing yourself. You taught me long ago that it's possible for anyone to make a change for the better and be a success. You are missed daily.

To my parents with love: Ransom and Caroline Yarnall and Fred Ferguson for giving me a sense of humor and self-confidence. Mom, thanks for cheering me on and supporting me through hard times as well as the good. I couldn't have done this without you. And to my grand-mother, Lois Post, for sitting me in front of the Olivetti and reading my first written words and believing in me—you will forever be my inspiration!

And to my "sisters," Julie Laubach, Valerie Fanning, Edwina Villegas, Cheryl Harper, Ciaran Clayton, Durenda Benton Tomczyk, Ladies with Gusto, and the GHS Lunch Ladies—we will always be friends no matter what! Thank you!

It is with a mother's love that I thank my talented and beautiful children, Aja Renee and Samuel Thomas, for their support and encouragement and for taking it in stride that I would succeed. No one loves their children more than I!

And finally, a few sappy words dedicated to the man who told me that I had the talent to be a writer and to go for it, my love: my husband, Ralph. To be able to still make me laugh every day no matter what is happening in the world around us is the greatest gift I will ever receive. I am grateful for every moment I spend with you, and when all those strangers tell me I'm lucky to be married to you, I have to admit: they're right. *Je vous aimerai toujours!*

Part One

Soul Searching:
What to Do After You Wipe Out

*"If you're not fired up with enthusiasm
you'll be fired with enthusiasm"*
—Vince Lombardi

So, you've been fired. Take a deep breath. Now let it out slowly. You packed your coffee mug and cleared your desk, feeling rejected, embarrassed, and freaked out over what happened. Okay, go ahead and stomp your feet if you have to, and shout, "Hey! It's not fair!" But be careful, or someone might call the cops. Being unemployed *and* in jail is not a good thing.

Even if you actually feel relieved—or thrilled because you'll never have to bust your butt for that place again—you still may feel like a loser without a job.

Being fired, or laid off, downsized, let go, or bought out sucks. You may panic that you won't have a place to go every day and your life won't have purpose. Your family and friends may worry, and paying $4 for a latte suddenly seems insane.

You might be concerned about paying the mortgage or for that overpriced SUV you bought when everything looked rosy. But trust us; in a few months you'll probably scratch your head and wonder why you even cared about that job. Really, what was so good about it anyway?

Maybe you slogged to the workplace for 8 to 10 hours a day carrying your lunch in a bag, working with people you wouldn't normally speak to, and you hated your boss. Come on, you can admit it. He or she was a jerk. Most are: that's why they're the boss. If you were the boss who just got canned, you were probably a jerk too. But here's your chance to start fresh. A do-over, if you will.

Losing your job is an opportunity to make changes. If you feel stagnant, we'll show you how to get moving again. You're actually in a great place. You may not have a job right now, but you have time for yourself. Stay in your pajamas and read this book. Accept the fact that you're unemployed and need to do something to make those car/house/tuition payments. You might find yourself browsing books about interviews, job searches, and boring reference crap. But wait! This is the book that will actually make a difference. Here you'll find ways to adapt your skills to a changing job market, the latest news on hot new industries, and advice from other people—just like you—who were fired and lived to tell about it.

Out of hundreds of fired people we interviewed, we picked the best, most outrageous stories of how spurned employees parlayed misfortune into the best time of their lives. Being fired turned out to be the greatest thing that ever happened to them. Some created "cage free" streams of income as freelancers. Others found new business opportunities and awesome careers they never imagined.

So don't put that uncomfortable suit back on just yet. Resist the temptation to interview for a job you'll end up hating. Instead, take time to read this book and find out how to live your passion, do what you love, and capitalize on new trends. We'll give you the resources, tools, and insights to rebrand yourself and find what's right for you. Making money is essential, but you also need a life. We'll help you to find a sense of adventure and purpose instead of a survival game.

Navigating your life and career is a lot like surfing—it's challenging, exciting, and unpredictable. Sometimes you soar, sometimes you wipe out. Life situations, like waves in the ocean, will always shift and change. This book will help you prepare for a shifting reality. Getting the most out of surfing—and life—depends on timing, readiness, attitude, and skill. Not knowing what's next after you lose your job is scary. We're here to help you *catch the wave* and *ride the pipeline* to new opportunities.

Read *Thank You for Firing Me!* and find out about other ways to live your life *and* make money. It can happen. Really. We've been fired from lucrative positions and gone without "real jobs." We not only survived, we discovered a whole new level of success. So have the other folks who have contributed their stories.

You'll find out about career and business opportunities in emerging markets both here and abroad, plus how to become an independent contractor. We know it takes time to find those reliable resources for hot new careers, but you now have plenty of time on your hands, right? This book is designed to help you figure out what's right for you. You'll also need time to find happiness and a way to create income. That's where we come in.

Surfing the next wave of success after you lose your job *can* be done. But it isn't easy. If you were standing on a surfboard for the first time out in the ocean, you'd most likely fall off the board. Your first objective is to feel the balance by adjusting your stance and approach. Before you jump back into the working world, you'll need to evaluate yourself and be willing to try new approaches to the changing job market. We'll give you tips on how to adapt your skills to a new career and stay motivated to find success. You may take a nose dive or float aimlessly for awhile. As you read this book, consider that there will be times you might need to watch and contemplate as each opportunity presents itself. Rather than force yourself to fit into a rigid set of goals and expectations, try developing a feel for new trends. Trends, like the tides, have a subtle momentum that moves you toward new discoveries. Luckily you picked up *Thank You for Firing Me!*, which will help you pick the *right* wave and help you to find a way to ride it in while guiding you through the next phase of your life.

So now that you've calmed down and actually started reading our book, you have begun the process. When you've finished reading our chapters we suspect you'll want to call your boss … and thank him or her for firing you.

CHAPTER ONE

Reconnect Before You Rebound

"Oh, you hate your job? Why didn't you say so? There's a support group for that. It's called EVERYBODY, and they meet at the bar."

—Drew Carey

"We're letting you go." These are words a boss might use to tell you to get out and please don't come back. If bosses could give you the whole truth, they'd probably say:

"Hey, it's not our fault you settled for the big paycheck instead of staying true to yourself while working for less money at something you love. And okay, you might have loved this job, but the fact is, we're not making enough profit to keep paying you. And, well, to be blunt, no matter how much you cared about this company, we don't really care about you. We care about our bottom line. If we have to downsize, we will. We'll do what it takes regardless of your situation. We don't want to give you money for being here anymore. We're setting you free. We don't need you."

Ouch!

Rejection, desperation, or the fact that you haven't read this book yet might send you reeling toward the next miserable job situation. Rebound jobs are like rebound relationships. If you take the next job that comes along, it will be a safety blanket to distract yourself from the pain for a short time, but if you're just surviving, things could go downhill quickly. We want you to find your soul first before jumping back into the water.

Killer Job or Job That Kills?

Gina was only 28 when she was made vice president of an accounting firm. "I worked 6 days a week, 10 to 12 hours a day, but I couldn't seem to please my manager, who I suspected was highly medicated," Gina said. "I never had time for anything beyond work. My job consumed me to the point that my relationship with my boyfriend ended and I lost my friends. Sad as it sounds, my job was my life."

When Gina's father suffered a stroke, she could only spare a weekend to fly across the country to his bedside, causing major conflict with her siblings. And here's the clincher: the money she earned wasn't even that big a payout. Gina was exhausted. Her health suffered and she was already plotting her exit when the ax came down.

"Truth is, I'd written my resignation letter and had established a hard quit date when they called me in to tell me they were 'letting me go,'" Gina explained. "I received two extra months to plan and implement my next life stage, which is what I wanted to do in the first place, and I received unemployment insurance. It was a huge relief not to work night and day crunching numbers. I finally had my life back."

Gina decided to leave the world of finance and became a freelance business writer. "Life is so much better now," she said. "I wake up in the morning happy. I exercise, have coffee, and work when I need to. Some days I work 10 hours and other days I work 2. It all balances out, and I can work from anywhere. Being fired was the best thing that ever happened to me."

"I couldn't seem to please my manager, who I suspected was highly medicated."

As a result of being fired, Gina learned to love her new career and her life. The money isn't predictable, but it works for Gina. Many people would have grabbed the next desk job that came along, with another difficult boss in the same suit making unreasonable demands, but Gina didn't. And neither should you.

Hey Driver, Follow That Bliss!

Consider the time it takes to get ready for work and travel there and back. You don't have to do that anymore. Add in the time you spent doing your job. Before you start working again, you have 50 or 60 more hours a week to think. You have time to be resourceful. You have time to explore ideas and consider things you never thought of before. You have time to give up some of your materialistic addictions and get real for awhile. You have time to find out how the people in your life feel about you. You're free to dream about who you really are. You're free to be honest with yourself. "We no longer require your service." Those words will make you stronger.

Now that you're *sans* job, you can begin to think about what's most important to you in life by concentrating on how to make a difference in this world. Think about what you can do personally that will count for something and therefore make you feel proud of yourself. If you're a creative person and you always wanted to paint, well, umm, "hello?" Now's the time. Are you passionate about taking photographs, making music, writing, or designing clothing? Well, guess what? You just were given a reprieve from a long sentence in purgatory.

> *"Being fired from the dot-com world was horrible for about a week. Since then I haven't looked back."*

"We're letting you go." Sweet! You're no longer in confinement. If you're a creative person, you've already realized that it's impossible to create in captivity. Even if you're not an artist, creative expression is a basic need for mental health. But there is a price to pay. You are now going to be forced to think about the truth of exactly who you are and what you can do to survive and thrive. The good news is you have the time. Time is power. You couldn't think about any of this before you were canned.

If It's Broken, Don't Fix It

"I was fired from my fourth dot-com job, and it led me into a completely different field," Mike said. "I took my first real vacation in 25 years, and I fell into the travel industry while I was in Florida. Now I manage a glass-bottomed boat business for a guy who has other companies and no time for this one. I work for someone else and I earn a paycheck with medical benefits, but it's almost like working for myself. Being fired from the dot-com world was horrible for about a week. Since then I haven't looked back."

Most people interviewed for this book decided to create a new path for themselves. They went from structure to no structure. They went from certainty (boredom) to uncertainty (a new adventure every day). They all, in a sense, were set free, just like Lauren who turned a bad experience into a thriving business.

"I'm now self-employed and grateful for every day, but I used to work for a medical supply company as an administrative assistant. I was miserable. My manager always came in late, gave me her work to do, spent most of the day talking with her boyfriend, and in general she was a really bad boss. One day I arrived first to the office and found a FedEx package waiting at the door, but it looked as if it had been through a war zone—partially opened and all beat up. I saw my name on the papers sticking out of the envelope. They were my termination papers!

I threw the package on my manager's desk and walked out. When I got home, I called the HR department and told them I was wrongfully fired. After a week-long investigation I was offered my job back, but I refused. I took the severance package they offered and went on to a much better career. I definitely moved on to greener pastures, now owning my own business helping others find new careers. I use this experience as a daily reminder of what *not* to do as a manager."

In this chapter, we'll coach you how to avoid "rebound" work—that is, settling for your next job simply for the money. We want you to figure out what you always wanted to do, what lights you up, what's missing in your life, and what you were meant to do. If you've been fired from every job you obtain, you may discover you're a unique person with something highly specialized to offer the world. Or possibly you have deeper issues. Either way, we want to help.

Liz Smith, the famous celebrity gossip columnist, in an interview with WomenForHire.com, related her experiences: "I lost every job I ever had. I've been fired so many times. I was fired from my first job selling hearing aids. These old people would come in and say their hearing aid batteries weren't working. I felt sorry for them and gave them free batteries, so I was fired for that. I had a great job at NBC as a producer and was fired from that because of the Eisenhower recession. I've left a few jobs, but usually I would get fired. Being fired from a job just means you're catapulted into another adventure."

Smith wrote for magazines from *Cosmopolitan* to *Sports Illustrated* before signing on as a syndicated columnist for the *New York Post*. Most important is what Liz Smith said she knows about herself: she loves reading and finding out what other people are doing. Every time she was fired, she had no indication she was destined to become a famous gossip columnist. But being fired brought her one step closer to what she truly loved to do.

What do you know about yourself? Some people don't know a thing about themselves and only discover who they are when the chips are down.

Being fired is a catalyst for change. It might motivate you to move to a different city where the lifestyle fits your personality. That's exactly what happened to Steve.

Put This in Your Pipe and Smoke It

Steve was a stressed-out mortgage broker for 15 years in New York. After being let go from the third bank he worked for, he started his own mortgage brokerage company.

"It didn't take me long to start making millions," Steve recalls. "I was living the life. I figured I had made it when I married Jennifer. She was beautiful, but still she talked me into spending $35,000 on plastic surgery." Steve and his beautiful wife worked hard. As the company grew, so did their workweek. They went from 40 hours a week to 70- and 80-hour weeks. The more money they made, the more they spent.

"A few years into the business we had six homes and six property tax bills that needed paying. It was stressful to think about, but the market was on fire and the money kept rolling in." Then the beginning of the loan crisis began to slow Steve's business in 2006. Steve put the homes up for sale. None of them sold.

"I went to bed every night with panic attacks and woke up in the morning with migraine headaches. Our sex life was over. When Jen filed for divorce I had a nervous breakdown. It was ugly." Steve thought the worst was over, but he was wrong. He was diagnosed with a brain tumor. "It turned out I needed surgery and chemotherapy. My only family lived in California, so I moved there for treatment. My doctors prescribed medical-grade marijuana to help me endure the effects of the chemotherapy. Until I moved, I had no idea cancer patients in some states could legally possess and smoke high-quality weed for pain." After surgery and chemo, Steve committed himself to a mental health institution. While he took time to recover, his homes went into foreclosure, and the business went bankrupt. Steve's therapist recommended he pinpoint what he honestly, authentically loved doing. Money couldn't be part of the equation. "My therapist told me to write a letter to someone important. I had to explain what it was I really wanted to do if obtaining money wasn't the goal."

Steve wrote a letter to his older brother: "Dear Dave. I always enjoyed helping people. While I was recovering, the only thing I could do was pour water on that potted plant next to my hospital bed. It reminded me of what I loved doing most. When I wasn't working or arguing with Jennifer, I was outside taking care of the garden, and I felt calm and happy."

Through writing his letter, Steve figured out what he loved to do and boiled it down to two things: growing plants and customer service. He acquired his California marijuana growers' license and a contract to cultivate medical marijuana for cancer patients. Steve now works 20 hours a week and volunteers another four in workshops with cancer patients. "Whenever people ask me what I do for a living, my answer always makes them laugh," Steve said. "Being a licensed marijuana grower makes me unique. I produce a product that's in demand—and legal with a prescription. Only in California do you hear this type of a success story."

> "Whenever people ask me what I do for a living, my answer always makes them laugh."

We're not saying you should move to California and cultivate marijuana, or become ill, or smoke pot. That's your business. We're saying that if you're faced with losing everything, that occasion is actually an ideal time in your life to do some radical soul searching to identify what's most important to you.

John McCrea is a managing partner at Bialla & Associates, a successful executive search consultant firm in Sausalito, California. He shares his insights for opening doors to a new economy job you will love.

"There are important core questions you should ask yourself before starting your job search," McCrea said. "But the first, 'What are you passionate about?' is probably the most important."

"This is the foundational question for being happy. It could be an industry—green, fashion, education, consumer products—or it could even be a function," he said. "Are you passionate about solving problems? Or it may be as simple as 'I am passionate about people and working with people.' Knowing what you love will help form your career direction."

McCrea balances his family and professional life on an even keel. In his spare time he plays basketball in the "Over 40" league, rows for the Marin Rowing Association's master's program, backpacks, and plays his guitar when he can squeeze it in. "You should definitely try to accommodate your passion into your life and, because your career is a big part of your life, you need to consider your career in the context of your passions," he said. "I know many people, for example, whose passion is their family. Their career or job is important in that it affords them the ability to support their family, but [it's] not necessarily their passion in and of itself. If you understand this, you will be happier in your eight-to-five job or career because you can connect it directly to your passion."

What Are You Good At?

McCrea suggests that, irrespective of your passion, you probably have learned what you are good at—and, just as importantly, what you are *not* good at. It could be that you are great with numbers or great with people. Regardless, focus on jobs that leverage your strengths and minimize your weaknesses.

What Are Your Goals?

"If your goal is to 'make as much money as possible,' you need to consider that in your job and career selection," McCrea said. "If your goal is to have 'a good work/life balance,' that also will influence your job and career focus. The simple discipline of answering these questions will help you determine where to focus your energy," he said. "The more you know yourself, the more directed you will be, and the more directed you are, the easier it is to find opportunities that fit." We'll look at more of McCrea's core questions in later chapters.

Go from Burnout to Big Time

You might have been fired from a job you loved. You might have once known what your goals and passions were, and what you were good at, but over time the excitement faded. In a competitive job market the chances of being replaced with someone who's more enthusiastic and willing to work for less money are pretty good. If you were burned out on your job but thought you hid it well, think again! People aren't as dumb as they look. Burnout can unconsciously send a message that you don't want to be there. Losing your job can be an opportunity to transfer your passions to a more interesting and rewarding format, and a chance to earn more money.

Paula, who lives in Los Angeles, started waiting tables in her teens. "By the time I was 32, I hated serving people. I went from loving the interaction to wanting to toss food in their faces."

Paula was fired from an upscale restaurant where she normally took home $200 to $300 in tips a night. "I loved banking the money, but loathed every minute I spent at work."

Paula began thinking about what drew her to the restaurant business in the first place. She thought of herself as a "people pleaser." To make sure she was right about herself, she took a personality test, and sure enough, the results stated she derived true pleasure from making people happy. But after a decade in the business, Paula knew she didn't want to please people by serving them food anymore. When she reflected on her first restaurant job, she identified it as a competitive business to break into without skills or experience, especially in Los Angeles, where waiting tables is the number one job choice for out-of-work actors.

Paula figured out a way to transfer her assets to a lucrative, exciting new business. She melded her success of serving people and 14 years of restaurant knowledge into one package. Using those skills, she embarked on a restaurant training business to help people break into the industry.

"It's harder to land a serving gig than an acting job," said Paula, who capitalized on a huge demand.

With no investment money, she convinced a restaurant owner to let her teach classes the one night they were closed. She taught her students how to wait tables and work behind the bar. "I paid the owner part of the fees I collected," she said. "I posted free advertisements on Craigslist, and 10 people registered the first week."

Paula charged $50 per class and made $500 in three hours explaining everything she knew. She paid 20 percent to the restaurant owner, who also benefited from the extra publicity. Now she gives four classes per week and earns $500 per class with a limit of 10 people per class. "My typical workweek is about 12 hours teaching and 8 hours putting up ads, making calls, and registering people. I usually earn about $2,000 per week, which translates to $8,000 per month," she said. "How great is that? I can double my income any time I want by setting up four more classes." Paula will never have to serve another plate of food again because she makes enough money to hire a caterer to serve her guests. "I love being a mentor, and I have plenty of contacts in the business. I refer students all the time to some of the best restaurants in L.A. My life couldn't have turned out better." Paula lives her passion and works fewer hours. She makes more money than she ever imagined, and she now earns enough to buy a decent health insurance policy and start a retirement fund.

Bulletproof Yourself

It's important to identify what actions and desires are meaningful. Meaningful actions are activities that produce real satisfaction right down to your core. Once you identify work you're passionate about, which gives you a deep sense of accomplishment, you can figure out a way to earn a paycheck. You can do what you're passionate about in any context, whether you end up as a business owner, independent contractor, or work for somebody else. If you do what comes naturally and it's work that you honestly love, you're bulletproof. Being bulletproof means that nothing will stop you from doing what feels right, even if you are fired. Your passion will always sustain you.

To find your next career, you first have to identify and connect with your true passion. If you're blocked, try some of these exercises career experts have recommended:

1. Write a letter (as Steve did) to the person who means the most to you. Answer at least one of the following:
    a. What did you dream of doing when you were a child? (Game show host? Fireman? Circus clown?)

b. What makes you feel calm and satisfied?

c. What makes you feel accomplished and proud of yourself?

d. If you could do anything you want and you didn't have to make money, what would it be?

2. Take a personality test to find out what kind of person you are and what type of career attracts you. (Explore PersonalityTest.net.)

3. Observe how it feels to do something you enjoy, and think about how to turn that into a career (as Paula did).

Brainstorming Tip

Write a short description of what you want, using your list to do some brainstorming.

Here's an example of brainstorming done by Eddie, a burned-out police officer from Indiana. Eddie wrote: "I get a rush from rescuing people. I want to work in different cities all over the country. I want to meet new people and be independent. I want a safe work environment. I want recession-proof job security."

Eddie is now working toward an online degree in nursing and is excited about his plans to become a traveling emergency room nurse. Later in this book we'll show you how to cross-reference your passions and skills with job descriptions compiled by the U.S. Department of Labor.

Help for the Perpetually Fired

Are you unemployable?

You've had a million different jobs—for about three weeks each. You've held every job there is, from mortician to insurance salesperson, and nothing seems to fit. If you *can't hold a job* to save your life, don't give up. Check out the resources to deal with ADD in the resource guide at the back of this book. You can try different things in a short period of time without commitment.

Seriously, what's going on inside your head? Are you restless? Do you have too much energy for a cubicle? Do you need a job where you run around outside all day? Are you really an artist who resists just going for it? In addition to brainstorming your list of passions and skills, it's especially important to know what isn't you and doesn't feel right. When you're brainstorming, compare your passions and skills with your list of dislikes and weaknesses.

"I really hated my job working for an insurance company," said Charlene. "I know that I didn't put much into that job. I didn't like it and I grew lazy, but they paid me a lot of money. When my boss let me go, I panicked. She explained that she knew I wasn't happy and that she could see it in my work, but still I was pretty upset that I had screwed up."

Charlene was miserable, but she wanted the paycheck. Sound familiar?

"I stayed home for weeks feeling sorry for myself, making half-hearted attempts at job hunting," she said. "Then I got a call from a former client who had my old business card with my cell number on it. He had a question, and I was the only one who knew the answer. Our conversation made me think about starting my own insurance brokerage company. I realized that I hated reporting to an office, but I liked working with clients and doing research to help them with their insurance needs. Five years later, I love my job and the unique way I've designed my work style. I spend six months a year working from home, and the other half of the year traveling in my motor home, working on the road. When I think back on how unfulfilled I was in that old job, I think my boss knew I had more to offer."

Be realistic and honest before taking on your next venture. If you were unhappy or in a job that wasn't right, your boss did you a favor. It may not seem like it now, or next week, but a few months down the road you'll thank us. We'll bet our careers on it.

In the next chapter, we'll coach you on how to use some of that precious time you now have to focus and think about what matters most to you.

CHAPTER TWO

Getting the Most Out of Drifting

"If you really want something in this life, you have to work for it. Now, quiet, they're about to announce the lottery numbers!"
—Homer Simpson

A s you think about the opportunities ahead, are you feeling a little nervous? Is the clock in your brain going tick-tick-tick? Do you feel impatient and anxious to make something awesome happen—*like right now*? Well, hang on a second. The cool thing about surfing is drifting. Before the swell of the next wave, there's a period of quiet calm; you appreciate where you are. You anticipate the excitement rumbling on the horizon. You're drifting with a purpose. As you float in tranquility, you're bracing for a wild ride when the time is right. Being out of work can cause you to feel lost and disconnected, especially if you're job hunting purely to survive unemployment. To regain a sense of control, shift your viewpoint to purposeful drifting. It's important to make the most of your down time between jobs or careers so you can re-enter the workforce powerfully and be prepared to take charge.

Before you bolt for that dream career, take full advantage of this ebb. When your days are free and unhurried you can enjoy a deeper connection to yourself by spending time with family, friends, hobbies, and whatever calms your soul.

Money problems and challenges are headed your way. Sorry for the reality check. In order for you to be focused, happy, confident, and geared for success, the way you spend your unemployment time needs to be tweaked.

Maybe slightly. Maybe significantly. Staying upbeat while you manage your time productively will be a challenge. But if you use this time to nourish your body, fortify your mind, and feed your soul, you'll catch the next wave of your career in the best shape of your life. You'll have the advantage over someone who spent his or her downtime panicked, depressed, and focused on fears. Who would *you* hire—a happy, confident person or someone who is miserable? People can smell desperation. So read on!

The Doctor Is In

David Peters is a family psychotherapist in San Diego, and he has shared his advice with us. Much of his work is with people in crisis from workplace harassment, job loss, and life transitions. Peters has counseled hundreds of people through the emotional upheaval of losing a job.

"Many people experience their workplace as a second home," Peters explained. "We spend so many hours there, giving our best, and often working with others in a team. Whether we like our job or not, the workplace is a place where we want to 'belong.' When we are among those who get laid off, it's easy to take it personally: 'They don't want me anymore. I don't get to be with them.' We often lose friendships when we leave. Remember that losing a job is a real loss and often results in real grieving, as if someone you know and loved has died. As with all grief, there is a time to indulge and a time to recover. Spend no more than a few days in your grief. Do it, and do it well. It's important to acknowledge the loss in order for your brain to process the change. Call the friends and family you need for support; do your crying or fretting or wondering why. Write out all your sadness, bitterness, or fear in a journal. Spend a day being quiet by yourself, if you you need to. And then . . . be done with it. It's time to move on. When a loved one dies, it's important to respond by being fully alive. And when we lose our job, it's important to respond . . . by working."

Working. Get it? Losing a job can lead to vulnerability and depression. The recently unemployed tend to sleep late, eat poorly, and sit alone in the house watching TV or wasting time playing video games. If you sink into a funk, you can start feeling better by taking some simple but effective actions, according to Peters. First, dedicate yourself to getting at least 45 minutes of good exercise five days a week. "Exercise will raise your serotonin levels as much as if you took 20 milligrams of Prozac. Most psychiatrists rarely tell their patients this, but clinical research has proven it," Peters told us. "It's best if you go out in the morning for a fast walk outdoors, in the sunlight, allowing about 15 minutes without sunglasses. Natural-light therapy also helps ward off depression and keeps your sleep/wake cycle intact," he said. "Many people who lose their jobs spend a lot of time in anger, cursing at their former employer, the economy, the government, and whomever. But anger is not going to help you now. Anger saps your brain of resources that you need for your current job— that is, looking for your new job. Anger increases your stress, sending cortisol (a stress hormone) into your bloodstream and throughout your body. This actually damages your coronary system and limits your brain's ability to think creatively. Catch your anger, take a few deep breaths, and shift your thoughts to the positive. For some people this takes practice, but it's essential. Positive thinkers are attractive to others and create more opportunities for themselves. And positive thinkers are more likely to see opportunities that others miss."

Experts such as Peters have a lot of great advice, and we loved gleaning it from him, but we realize that getting over job loss is often easier said than done, particularly for anyone who takes rejection hard. After you indulge your inner bummed-out, unemployed person, it's time to stop complaining and think about new adventures and possibilities. Bottom line: the road to recovery is being responsible for your future. To make your journey back to work realistic, separate yourself from your circumstances. Try not to define yourself by your employment status. Devote this chapter to you, and view our suggestions as a strategy to build up yourself.

Better Mind, Better Body

Arnoux Goran, founder of Total Health Mastery, a health education and seminar program, spoke to us about ways to process negative emotions after losing a job: "Take some time to deal with your stuff, give yourself a break, and have some fun. Then, the most empowering thing you can do for yourself is to reach a point where you can feel complete with your old job, and be ready to create what's next."

Goran offers specific techniques you can use to empower yourself, clear negative emotions, and achieve new goals in his book, *The Seven*

Steps to Reprogramming Yourself, which is available in e-book format at THmastery.com.

"To achieve a sense of closure about getting fired, and be complete about the past, first you'll need to clear out your old emotions," he said. "Step one is getting present to your negative feelings. To do this, think of what is bringing up the feelings, like the fact that you got fired, and then answer the following question: if this feeling could talk, what would it say? Keep asking the feeling what it would say until your response is totally gone and there's nothing left to say. Write it all down. Your answers tell you what your core beliefs are behind your emotion. It's important to know what your core beliefs are that lead you to feel bad. You need to know what they are first before you can clear them."

Goran understands the joy of comforting your broken heart with food, but he warns us that this will delay your success. Next time you order a personal pizza with extra pepperoni, work on clearing your emotions first. "If you keep stuffing your emotions with food and you don't clear what you need to deal with, then you'll attract whatever you're feeling. That's the law of attraction. So it's important to clear those feelings. For example, say you lose your job and become very afraid you won't be able to pay your bills. If you continue to stay in that fear, you'll be paralyzed. You'll eat more food instead of taking action. You'll actually *attract* not being able to pay your bills. At the very least you have to get out of that space, and you need to clear those feelings permanently or they'll come back. If you don't clear it today, you'll re-create it tomorrow."

Pessimistic thinking may seem justified, but when you allow it to run your actions, it attracts the very thing that you dread. Dedicate yourself to practicing positive programming and self-talk on a daily basis. Doing so is your inoculation against hopelessness and a loss of power. Give yourself space to process feelings of doubt, confusion, fear, or anger. If that annoying voice in your head doesn't stop hammering you with negative thoughts, explore UrbanMonk.net, a comprehensive Web site filled with postings to read that help train your mind to work through buried emotions, think constructively, and stop negative thinking. Some of their best articles talk about purging built-up energies such as denial and repression and how to master your emotions. The site also features a series of articles to help you face fear, insecurity, frustration, sadness, doubt, and anger.

Eliminate Blame

Blame is a time waster that depletes vitality. You become the victim of the person or circumstance you blame for the cause of your situation. Finding fault with others weakens you. Blamers don't create results. They can't create, because blame has made them powerless. Don't play the blame card.

Own Your Actions

To boost your personal power and confidence, think about the weeks that led up to the day you were fired. Think about a bad situation you experienced that seemed unfair. Identify specific things you did or said and what your attitude was during that time period. Be ruthlessly honest—but don't beat yourself up; that's blame. Taking responsibility for your actions is acknowledging what your role was that led to your current situation. Admitting your part in the end result is owning your actions. Being responsible is not self-blame.

For example, Carol, a programmer who was fired after 15 years on the job, was tempted to blame her male coworkers. She felt the men in her office were allowed to make more mistakes. Even if it were true, there was another part of the picture for which Carol took responsibility.

"If I had to 'tell one' on myself, I know I was burned out on the work. I was good at what I did, but I didn't update my skills or take any courses on the latest information in my field," she said. "My coworkers who got promotions were always going the extra mile." The instant Carol recognized her role in the end result of being out of a job, she didn't feel like a victim. "When I admitted to myself that my attitude was a contributing factor, I felt freed. I was excited about taking classes to update my skills and look for a new job."

Why does recognizing your role in the end result give you power? Acknowledging your actions is being responsible for what you think, say, and do. Being responsible requires courage and strength. Power arises from courage and shows up as confidence. When you own your actions, you own confidence. You feel sure of yourself, even if you screw up. Sure, some circumstances you can't control, like a crappy economy, but the ability to distinguish what you can be responsible for gives you access to trusting yourself and your future.

In the resource section of this book, you'll find some popular personal development programs, Web sites, and publications. For DVDs and success seminars, check out StudyWithJack.com.

Eating well is more important now than ever. Specific foods you eat can affect your mood and brain chemistry. If you can't afford to shop at fancy health food stores right now, look for fresh fruit and vegetables at your local farmer's market or grocery store. Some health food stores and co-ops sell organically grown produce at reasonable prices. Add nuts and grains to your diet, which provide protein, essential fats, and B vitamins to nourish your brain and nervous system, and stay away from the soda, fast food, and copious amounts of caffeine and booze. For more information about foods and nutrients that improve your mood, visit MoodCure.com. Get some decent rest, even if you're not waking up to leave for work in the morning. Make sure you go to bed at the same time every night as if you were still working, and wake up at the same time each morning. Why? Because you have a job to do! You are now employed full time at the tasks of job seeking, skills training, and professional networking.

Don't let yourself go because your company let you go. Take advantage of your time to exercise, not only for being a happier person but to look better. Jump back into the job market feeling comfortable in your own skin. Get out of your sweatpants—it's time to get dressed. As we previously mentioned, don't quit working out. If you can handle the payments, keep the gym membership. Belonging to a gym gives you a reason to go out every day, a place to watch the news if your cable has been turned off, and a place to shower if you didn't pay the water bill. You can also see your friends, not to mention stay in shape. Yoga classes are perfect for stress; if you can't spring for classes, buy a yoga DVD. Walk to the park and practice Tai Chi with other people or join a local biking club to get the blood pumping. Whatever it takes to get you moving, do it! It's essential to breathe right now and get the oxygen flowing to your brain so you can think clearly about your situation and prepare for opportunities.

If you can, keep getting haircuts. If you color your hair to stay younger looking, keep that gray touched up; just don't get the hair styling at the five-star salon where a cut and color is the same price as a plane ticket to Paris. Check out places like Supercuts, Fantastic Sams, and especially your local cosmetology school. Here's a little secret: if the students at the school mess up your hair, the instructor usually fixes it for free. Until your life gets back on track, it's important to resist the temptation to completely ignore your body and soul in the name of penny pinching. What you will save on gym fees and salon costs will go to medicine and doctor's bills if you don't feel good about yourself during this stressful time.

Time Revisited

Here's a question to ponder: if you knew your own ultimate deadline—the exact day of your death—how much would you value the time left? Yeah, we know, buzz kill, but face it, you will die eventually. The problem is you don't know when your time will be up. Death could come calling while you read this book. (We hope it doesn't!) Spending too much time pursuing money is just wrong. Trying to accumulate more toys than your neighbor has nothing to do with happiness, but spending time with people you love and even yourself has everything to do with contentment and well-being. Too often, the pursuit of money—or the lack thereof—can derail time, true purpose, and happiness. It won't be easy, but staying upbeat and taking advice from family, friends, experts, and us while you are looking for work is key to attracting positive job opportunities into your life.

No Time for Dying

Paul, a harried stockbroker from San Francisco, found out he had less than six months to live when doctors found a tumor and diagnosed cancer. It was a wake-up call to a workaholic. He was driven to make the most of the time he had left. "I quit my job, stopped paying my mortgage, and dug into my 401(k) so I could treat myself and friends to everything I'd always wanted to do but couldn't because of my career," Paul said. He was usually too busy to even attend family gatherings. "It was sad to be dying, but somehow it was the best time of my life. And that was the point. Before, I kept waiting until I reached certain goals to take time off or have fun with people, but that time never came. My life was all about money. I was kind of an ass. When death was calling my name, money suddenly didn't seem important."

For six months Paul traveled to places like Belize and Paris. He visited the Grand Canyon with his nephews and drank Heinekens in Amsterdam with his new girlfriend. "I pretty much spent everything I had. Every penny. It felt great, but life was bittersweet because I realized I was going to die and my whole life until then had been focused on work. I only wished I could have more time to spend with my friends and family."

Six months after his death sentence, Paul received his wish. "Apparently the Grim Reaper hadn't called my name after all," he said. "The doctors gave me the wrong diagnosis. They assured me I was in good shape. They said they were very sorry. I wasn't." Paul had depleted his bank account and almost lost his home. He didn't care. "The house is for sale, and I'm looking for a new career. I'll probably get back into trading on the Internet from home, but that's it. The doctors were afraid I was going to sue, but they gave me a gift without even realizing it. I have a new outlook on life. It was an expensive lesson, but the price of dying without really living is even more costly."

> "It was an expensive lesson, but the price of dying without really living is even more costly."

Doctors aren't perfect. Misdiagnosed illnesses occur all the time. Luckily, you don't have to go through a medical roller coaster ride to understand the tricks your mind plays on you while working your butt off at a demanding job. Before you begin your search for work, consider how it will impact your personal life and your relationships. Trading excessive amounts of time and energy for the pursuit of money and material possessions can seriously jeopardize not only your health but also your connection to family and friends.

Misery Loves Company

Americans have plenty of reasons to be cranky, but, looking back, today's economic dilemma is not as bad as it seems. Have you ever heard of the U.S. Misery Index? It was created by economist Arthur Okun, an advisor to President Lyndon Johnson in the 1960s. It is simply the unemployment rate added to the inflation rate. It is assumed that a higher rate of unemployment and a worsening of inflation both create economic and social costs for a country. A combination of rising inflation and more people out of work are byproducts of deterioration in economic performance and a rise in the misery index. The fallout from our economic meltdown is considerable, but the misery index isn't even close to what it was in the late 1970s and early 1980s. In fact, we lived through much worse times and didn't even know how horrible it was! (There was no Internet back then, perhaps the key to our blissful ignorance.)

In the spring of 2009, when the U.S. unemployment rate was 8.6 percent, the Harris Poll Happiness Index concluded that 35 percent of Americans were very happy. Considering the unemployment rate and the gloom and doom being shouted from every rooftop, those were pretty good numbers. Nine in ten Americans agreed that their relationships with friends bring them happiness and they have positive relationships with family members. Eight in ten agreed that they were generally happy with their lives. The study also revealed that money doesn't always buy happiness. In fact, the group with the biggest smiles on their faces was the group making between $50,000 and $74,999 (39 percent), leaving behind the group making $75,000 and more (36 percent). This is evidence that even in hard times people are chipper. Unemployment didn't seem to be depressing them as much as the news would have us believe. Having a close network of friends and positive relationships with family members is what got them through the rough patches. It's clear to us that average Americans are *not* completely and horribly unhappy. They may be frustrated with certain aspects of their lives, and job loss is one of those aspects. The great news is that the rest of their lives seem to be going well. Remember: a happy person is the one who finds a new and rewarding job!

We have innumerable friends in our lives who have recently lost their jobs. They're using their unemployed days to figure out how to cut back on expenses, dust off their small business ideas, or get started on the Great American Novel. Hell, *we* started researching this book the instant we got canned from our jobs. This is your chance to figure out what's important to you and accomplish whatever you couldn't when you were busy working. This is an excellent time to dream and design your future. A lot of people are struggling right now. Even our rich friends are feeling some pain. Wealthy people in almost every sector ranging from the movie business to New York high society have lost bundles of money. But the climate is perfect for creative ideas and making connections. Businesses are open to trying new approaches now that they're feeling the pinch of what isn't working and what isn't selling. Just keep reminding yourself that you're not alone—keep up your friendships and things will turn around.

Drifting with a Purpose Is Good!

Valerie was let go from a large recruiting firm, but she refused to let it get her down. "The truth is I was very unhappy there. That said, I refused to panic or get discouraged about my lack of income. Instead, I followed my inner entrepreneur. I was thinking about becoming self-employed for a few years, and getting let go created just the opportunity I needed."

Valerie took her skills that she used at her former place of employment and put them to work for herself. "I started my own networking and career counseling business. I chose this because during my time as a recruiter, I found that the part of the job I really liked was when I was working with candidates and counseling them on their career. I focus on networking in my practice because so many people need to understand that in order to get what they want in their career, they *must* network. I love what I am doing now, and I feel as though I have finally listened to that little voice inside. I get to work from home and I wake up every morning refreshed and ready to take on the world. It is the perfect design for my life."

Planning your life much like Valerie did, based on identifying your strengths and building on them, should be your goal when you finish this chapter. You will rediscover who you are and what you really want in a job or career. Along the way, look for chances to have enjoyable experiences and think about aspects of your life that you truly appreciate. Feeling solidly related to yourself and others will help you achieve a confident connection with the person who is interviewing you for a job. If you strike out on your own as a consultant, freelancer, or entrepreneur, the power to connect will definitely be your most valuable tool.

Ways to Boost Your Relatedness

- Reconnect with old friends or relatives you haven't seen in a long time. The longer, the better. If you've had very good friends from college, high school, or elementary school with whom you've lost touch, try to find them on Facebook and talk about old times.
- Reminisce about adventures and mishaps you have had. Notice the way you feel while you're recalling your adventures. Think about how your days were before you became busy and caught up chasing the money.
- Organize a family reunion. Keep the conversation steered to remembering old times. If Grandma starts telling your dad she wishes he could be more like his successful brother, ask Grandma about her childhood and if she ever got into any mischief. If you've heard the story a million times, fish for more stories.
- Feel the pleasure of relating stories of happier times to others. Share your stories about the "good old days," and invite people to tell theirs.
- Remember a disastrous adventure you can now laugh about.

While you prepare yourself for the next phase of your life, use this time to create happiness. We're not telling you to be happy just so you won't whine and annoy your friends. Happiness is a powerful, attractive energy. People gravitate toward it. They want some of what you have to rub off on them.

We're in changing times, and the waves of change are rolling your way. Before you dive into the next chapter, think about how you'll be strengthening your mind and body. Appreciate the value of your personal relationships and your support network. And sharpen your ability to connect with people and achieve happiness. Using your unemployment time to empower yourself will prepare you for adapting your skills to upcoming trends and opportunities. So grab that surfboard, power up, and hang ten. Get ready. Here comes change!

Ways to Create Happiness

- Think about everything you're grateful for. Gratitude creates happiness.
- Think about your strengths instead of weaknesses.
- Explore types of work where you can build on your strengths rather than try to fix your weaknesses.
- Smile at a baby, and watch the baby smile back at you. Note how you feel, and remember you once used to be that easy to please.
- Align your thoughts and feelings toward the presence of happiness. This will motivate you. Be inspired.

CHAPTER THREE

How to Ride the Tides of the Changing Job Market

*"Ch-ch-Changes. Just gonna have to be a different man. Time
may change me. But I can't trace time."*

—David Bowie

The common dream of earning a college degree, walking into a high-
paying job, and owning a McMansion with a swimming pool and a
six-car garage has come to an end. You might have recently found yourself being squeezed out of a career with no retirement benefits or graduating from college and no one but your mom interested in that pretty
diploma.

In the past, success had been equated with material wealth for many
Americans: bigger and gaudier houses, long-term jobs with fat pensions,
giant SUVs, and cheap gasoline. By God, that was the natural born right
for everybody. But economic trends and cycles change throughout history.
When the job market changes, so must you. By changing your focus
from yesterday's consumer-driven climate to the next trend of building
and finding new niches, you'll be better suited for success.

"They" say people hate change, but what do "they" know? How
many times have you changed your hairstyle? Remember that ridiculous
mullet you sported in the 80s? How about clothes? You've gone from
wearing stonewashed jeans and stained T-shirts to suits and blazers.
Change. Have you been divorced? Changed the paint in your kitchen,
along with the tile? Change and change again. You've been doing it
forever without a second thought. It's a natural part of life. Of course,

you didn't expect to lose your job. That was a huge, unexpected, panic-inducing change. It may have hit you right upside the head, but you can—and will—recover. So let's see what we can do to get your life back under control. And if you still have that mullet, go get a haircut.

Imagine it's 1992 and you're trying to explain the concept of the Internet to corporate executives who can't grasp the idea of ideas flowing back and forth through a series of computers and thin air. While we can't promise our ideas will be as big as the next dot-com boom, they may get you started on a new career that makes you money and at the same time happy. How's that for change?

People tend to get stuck at various points in a career path and resist all efforts to change. It can happen when anyone is in a comfortable workplace that fails to stretch him or her professionally as well as in relationships and other aspects of his or her life, but it's important to change this particular way of thinking. You may feel that with the way things are, economically speaking, there's nothing you can do and it's a bad time to start over career-wise. You've heard it again and again; every position out there has 1,000 people applying for the opportunity. There are just too many people out there who are unemployed at the moment, but honestly that's just the attitude that you need to change. There *are* open positions and business opportunities out there, *right now*. Those jobs will be filled by people who persist and approach these prospects with a willingness to change and a progressive attitude. You have to maintain a sense of optimism and humor about your future. It sounds trite, but it works. The staggering competition you face for the job of your dreams won't go away anytime soon, but if you make a conscious effort to adapt your strengths to the arising demands of current market trends, you'll stand a much better chance of becoming gainfully and happily employed.

Here's Crystal's story:

"A few years ago I was terminated from my job. I was a computer trainer with a law firm. My training manager was hired about 10 months after me, and from the beginning he didn't like my style of training or my personality. We were a large law firm, and he was hired to add more trainers to help. He went on to hire nine more trainers who thought exactly like him and agreed with him consistently. One thing about me that is a liability: I'm not diplomatic. So when he asked a question and asked for everyone's "honest" opinion—I gave it to him. Of course when he was told he needed to terminate one person to stay in budget, it was an easy decision for him. I thought about ways to use my communication style to fill a need and decided to start my own business. I love helping others and had heard of coaching. The need for life and business coaching seemed to come with the rise of new entrepreneurs and small businesses. I found a school in New York to attend and became a certified coach. I knew then that being a coach was my destiny. I'm now a certified life coach who helps small business people with their technology branding and computer needs. I love to support professionals and help them evolve in the business world."

"I knew then that being a coach was my destiny."

The Japanese have a concept called *"Wabi Sabi,"* or the art of imperfection. A simple translation means: nothing lasts forever, nothing is ever completed, and nothing is perfect. Being stuck is part of the process of life. Don't take it personally. You may be thinking that the situations of life are permanent, pervasive, and personal. Although you may feel all of those things, it's not the case. Change is constant, and it accelerates if you actively pursue it. There are areas of your life that may not be perfect but are still good. Being unemployed, especially in this economy, isn't personal. The first thing to do when searching for a new career path is to acknowledge that you're imperfect. Maybe, embrace it. Better yet, take it out to dinner.

Brain Clutter 101

How do you change from stopped to unstoppable? One way to become mobile is to rethink old ideas that clutter your brain, keeping you in a rut. Do you really believe you're not smart enough for a new career? Do you think you need to be thinner to find a new job? Forget about it. Reinforce positive ideas that will shift your energy to a new career, in spite of what your friends tell you.

Pick a Card!

What can you do if time and money are limited? An inexpensive, fun way to train your mind is by using card decks from HayHouse.com. The site offers beautiful, artistically designed decks of cards inscribed with quick and easy bites of wisdom.

Some card decks for re-creating yourself:

SARK's Creative Dream Game

We all have creative dreams, however, life often clutters the pathways of those dreams. The Creative Dream Game is a fun and insightful way to release those dreams and clear the pathways to understanding.

The Four Agreements, by Don Miguel Ruiz

Based on Don Miguel Ruiz's New York Times best-selling book The Four Agreements, the 48 cards in this deck provide a simple, yet powerful, code of conduct for attaining personal freedom and true happiness.

Empowerment Cards: A Card Deck by Tavis Smiley

Talk-show host and author Tavis Smiley pours his passion for promoting positive change into these 50 personal-empowerment cards. Tavis's firsthand testimonies and words of wisdom will help you make critical decisions, allowing you to enhance both your own life and the lives of those in your community.

Power Thought Cards

Each vibrant card contains a powerful affirmation on one side and a visualization on the other to enlighten, inspire, and bring joy to your life.

Tips for Daily Living Cards

New York Times best-selling author Iyanla Vanzant has created the Tips for Daily Living card deck to help you address some critical life issues. Each card presents a question for you to consider, which, when answered honestly, will support you in creating a new personal vision.

Most of us feel reluctant when we take a risk and embark on a new occupation. Clinging to the same trite ideas about careers may seem safe, but in this day and age, is anything safe? What you should do to calm your nerves is create an action plan. Try not to take yourself too seriously, or this won't be any fun. Break down your plan into both goals you can reach in a year or less and goals you want to reach in five years or less. Don't hold back. Do whatever it takes to make your action plan entertaining. Call it your master plot for world domination, if you have to. Dive into this book, search the Internet, attend retraining seminars, and volunteer for internships for in-house training and thoroughly research what you'd like to do as a way to support yourself. Explore the risks and rewards so you'll have data for an informed decision.

If you're still doubtful about the steps you should take, write down every idea you come up with, no matter how wild or unrealistic. Sometimes the zaniest ideas are the best. Tackle one thing at a time. Discuss your plans with someone else. A fresh perspective can help you see things you may have missed before. Because we're all unique, variable experiences and thought processes along with different approaches can lead to alternative solutions. Psychologists tell us the human brain needs constant and ever-changing stimulation. The brain becomes bored once it masters a task or concept, and it wants to move on. If you don't want to tackle something new and different, maybe you actually need to. Staying in the same game for too long may account for the dissatisfaction so many people report in their careers. You're more adaptable than you think.

Think about your great-grandparents. Did they live through the Depression and make it? Were they in World War I or II and lived to tell about it? Those who have gone before us lived through upheavals so great we may never appreciate the strength and spirit they needed to survive. History shows that we humans are remarkably flexible and can adapt to a wide variety of situations and environments. Realizing this will encourage you to embrace change rather than avoid it.

Before you read on, try this quick exercise: Picture yourself about 10 years old. You're at a big family get-together. Aunt So-and-So asks you what you want to be when you grow up. You, as a 10-year-old say, "I want to be a _____."

Think about your answer. Does it still apply? If you wanted to be a cowboy, maybe you should be working with animals or become a trail guide, or, at the very least, you should work outside. Did you want to be a doctor but never went to medical school? Perhaps now is the time to go into a nursing program or apply at a health clinic. In reality you've always known what you wanted to be when you grew up. You just became side-tracked. Now you can finally be that kid again while earning a paycheck. We are raised being told we should be this or should do that. In the end, there is no "should," only "want to" and "decide to."

Go with the Flow

So here's the million-dollar question: should you only have one career in your lifetime? Was the career you had in your early and mid-20s the same as you have now? You've probably changed, so why hasn't your career? If you treat it like a lifetime commitment and you are fired or laid off, we can see why it's such a big deal. But should it be? The happiest people we know are the ones who get that and change careers every 5 or 10 years.

Dale was in the television business, working as a prop master for a long-running comedy show. After nine years the show was canceled, and Dale wasn't sure if he wanted to move on to another production. "It seemed glamorous working in TV, but it was just a job and I'd been doing it since I was 16," Dale said. "I worked strange hours. I stood around and did nothing while filming was underway. It was boring." Dale felt he was destined for a new career, but he didn't know which direction to pursue. He spoke to his friends who thought he was crazy to give up a job in TV, so he sought the help of a career counselor. "She had me write down what was important to me during this chapter of my life," he said. "I wrote the environment was important. Doing something that inspired me was important, but I didn't want to start from scratch." In the end Dale and his two brothers who were both in the construction business decided to build custom "green" homes. "With my background in set design and their experience in construction, everything came together. It was the right time. I think if I'd found myself out of a job a year earlier, I might have gone into the next TV production. Talking with a professional made me comfortable with my decision."

Put Me in Coach

Discovering your true passion and the job that will fulfill it may be hard to do on your own. A life coach or career coach can help you get unstuck if you're willing to invest the money. Prices vary depending on the format and person with whom you're working. Consulting a personal life coach can range from $75 to more than $200 per hour.

Ron was surprised when a coach helped him find that his ideal job was nothing like the one he'd been fired from. He saw the writing on the wall at his job, so he decided to be proactive and take matters into his own hands and find a coach.

"I was working for a Long Island bus company when our manager was forced out and a new manager was brought in. He wanted to have his own people, so he began to make our lives miserable. One by one we fell until I was the last one. I decided that I would not let the job affect me but to hold on as long as possible until I found something better. I worked with my life coach on finding a career that I was passionate about. In a discussion he asked my advice about a friend who was going through a divorce since I had raised my son very successfully as a custodial dad since he was a baby. He let me talk for about 45 minutes before interrupting me and said, 'I think we found your passion!' I created an organization called Single Parent Power. The mission is to empower single-parent families and reconnect them as a family through the use of workshops, retreats, and coaching individuals. Now I have an amazingly rewarding career with great successes of how I reconnect families."

Maybe now is the time for you to seek advice from a career counselor—FindYourCoach.com is a great site—or others, such as mentors or professionals in your support group. Many of your friends and family will want to help and encourage during these rocky times, and their support can make you feel connected, which is very nice of them. But you don't need comforting at this stage. You need to take charge of your fate and get out of your rut. This is a huge lesson for you: to grow. It's not a fun lesson but a lesson all the same. Look yourself straight in the eyes and accept responsibility while mustering the courage to take action. Control what you can, and get rid of the rest. You are in charge of you. Don't "hope" that something will happen, *make* something happen.

Life is full of surprises. It almost never goes in the direction you think it will. As a result, you should take the paths as they come. It's an exciting time to be alive, and eventually you will find that great job about which you have always dreamed. Yes, it will take time and it will take commitment, but you can do it. The times they are a-changin'—just make sure you change too!

How to Be Powerful:
REEDUCATION FOR REINVENTION

*"The last time I got fired my boss said, 'It's not me ...
it's you.'"*
—*Jackie Maruschak, stand-up comic*

Create an awesome you, and an awesome career will follow. Are you ready to reinvent yourself? If your answer is *yes*, you are now an agent of change. If you first reinvent yourself, you can then change the world. In the paragraphs that follow, you'll discover how to create a career that accurately expresses who you are as a unique individual. You will learn how to educate yourself from the inside out. You will uncover your true purpose and passion. When you follow your passion, you can find or create ways to profit from it. We'll give you some fun exercises to help you tap into work that lights you up. With these tools, and a bit of radical honesty, you'll have access to ways you can re-create yourself as a person who does what you love. You can take more risks and go for what feels right. You'll be able to attract people who support and further your intentions. Many of us will reinvent ourselves during our career, but where do we begin, and how is it done?

Rearrange Your Molecules

Goals are important if you are ready to reinvent yourself. Commit to one goal a day. Go someplace completely different from where you usually go during your routine. Don't go to the same Starbucks where they know you. Find a new café. Read a book. Read *this* book. Call someone you haven't spoken to in a while. Exercise each day, whether it's a walk on the beach or a heavy workout in the gym.

These small steps will create a new perspective, which can propel you into positive action. The trick is to *move!* Action creates more action. By doing something every day, you will slowly be moving in a different direction.

Weekend seminars, workshops, and informational CDs or DVDs aimed at helping transform old ways of operating are excellent means for getting "out of your head" and creating new possibilities. Landmark Education is one of the world's rapidly growing education corporations offering tools for creating breakthroughs. For a full description of their weekend seminar, The Landmark Forum, visit LandmarkEducation.com. To give you an idea of what the course offers in terms of change, here's a blurb from their Web site:

"Whenever we're limited in life, there is something—a context or framework—that we are blind to that is holding that limitation in place. Landmark's technology allows you to create breakthroughs in a two-step process in which you:

- "Uncover and examine the blind spots or context holding you back in your life.
- "Find out where your current context originated and address it for what it really is.

"Having completed these two steps, a new realm of possibility is available to you. The constraints from the past disappear. Your view of life, your thoughts, your feelings, and your actions, change—and the change is immediate, dramatic, and without effort. It is a breakthrough."

The benefits Landmark Education reports as a result of taking the course include the freedom to be absolutely at ease no matter where you are, who you're with, or what the circumstance, and the power to take action effectively in areas that are important to you. We recommend you check it out. Courses such as Landmark can provide a push to get you through the process. The point is: most of us get stuck in riptides at one time or another. Giving yourself a new mindset will help you seize new opportunities with confidence.

What's Missing?

Are there "holes" in your life where your skills and experiences don't connect with your passions and dreams? Try this "bridging" exercise to brainstorm and explore possible jobs that connect your skill (what comes naturally to you) to your passion (what you love like crazy) and your burning desire.

Jot down a list with the following categories:

Skills   Burning desire
Passion   What's missing?

List everything you can think of under each category without trying to analyze too much. List your skills, everything you are capable of doing, and your burning desire. Then look at the list and figure out what's missing; in other words, if you are honest with your list, would it put you on a course toward doing what you love?

This exercise is designed to help you figure out how to use your skills and your passions to finding the kind of work you love. By figuring out what's missing, you determine what you need to learn and where and how you can gain experience. Here's an example of how a fired sales rep benefited from this exercise:

Tiffany re-created herself when she switched her career from a burned-out sales rep to a special effects makeup artist at a major film studio. Here's how she used the brainstorm lists:

Skills: "I can talk to people, convince them I have good ideas. I can sell cosmetics. I'm patient. I don't give up easily. I have a creative imagination. I know how to put makeup on people. I can draw. I can sculpt little monsters and creatures out of modeling clay. I'm a stickler for details. I can sew. I can make my own Halloween costumes. I'm a pretty good hustler."

Passion: "I love monsters, horror movies, science fiction, and comic books. I love Halloween! Creating outrageous costumes gives me a rush. I like working with my hands."

Burning desire: "To make money using my imagination! How cool would that be? I'd gleefully spend the whole day working with my hands creating something from my imagination."

What's missing?: "A job that allows me to use my imagination. Experience working in a creative field. Knowing what to do with my passions. Training for a creative job as a designer of . . . Halloween costumes? Movie monsters? Fantasy outfits? A more fun way to work with makeup other than selling it to retailers."

> *"I love Halloween! Creating outrageous costumes gives me a rush."*

Bridge to Your Dream Job

Tiffany identified her passion and discovered what was missing in her life. She selected one key point from each list and linked the points together to find a career that excited her:

Sales + people person + makeup + imagination + sci-fi and horror movie obsession = special effects makeup artist

What's missing? For Tiffany: knowing how to apply special effects makeup, experience, and money to learn the trade.

After researching the special effects makeup field and talking with someone in the job placement department at a special effects makeup school in Los Angeles, Tiffany applied for student loans and signed up for a program that would provide her with the necessary qualifications.

Her student loans covered most of her tuition and housing expenses. For extra income, she freelanced at photography studios doing makeup for actors who needed headshots. Later she teamed up with a photographer and started a "fantasy photo portrait" business, where Tiffany transformed her customers with an exotic fantasy look using costumes and makeup.

Chances are you've met or heard of people who turned their passion into a career. Contact them and ask them how they did it. You might find out it's easier than you imagined. Start by thinking about your obsessions, hobbies, subjects you love to talk about at parties, and the kinds of magazines or Web sites you're compelled to visit for clues.

Find People and Ask Questions

Joining a local meet-up group in your area of interest is a fast way to make connections with people who can share information with you about professions in which you are interested. Getting out, meeting people, and drinking a glass of wine will be good for your soul. And these people will know other people. You'll network and make friends at the same time. Make sure to develop friends in different fields and in different generations. Web sites such as Meetup.com have groups for almost every subject and interest. Membership is free, and you can join as many groups as you want—or organize your own group for a small fee.

Tools to Apply Your Skills to Different Industries

Most of us are too narrow in our thinking about our skills and possible employers. There are more possibilities out there, but you have to look for them. The "turning lemons into lemonade" approach can be applied to adapting your product or service to a new market, or transferring your skills to a different industry. Make the most of these tools:

Resumes	Training	Pro bono work
Recruiters	Volunteer/internships	Online job markets

The resume is crucial. A savvy recruiter can help you write a killer one that showcases your qualifications. There are different styles of resume writing. No matter which you choose, your objective is to influence employers and convince them you can make their lives brighter.

If you post a resume online and you attract a recruiter, request tips on how to flesh out your resume with the appropriate details for the companies your recruiter will market you to. The following sites are some of the many places where you can find recruiters and list your resume: FindARecruiter.com, HeadhuntersDirectory.com, and TheRecruiterNetwork.com. If you think you have what it takes to start your own recruiting business, check out StartARecruitingBusiness.com.

Interviewing

We've had plenty of interviews over the years, and we're really good at that stage of the game, but we're going to go back to John McCrea, partner at Bialla & Associates, and ask him to share his advice:

> I find that the best interview techniques are just common sense (dress well, make eye contact, etc.). That said, these are in my opinion the most important things to keep in mind.
>
> **Do your homework.** Try the product; sign up for the service; Google the company and learn everything you can about them and take mental notes to use in the actual interview. It will indicate that you care and are passionate about the opportunity and will make your interview conversations that much more dynamic.
>
> **Listening is (much) more important than talking.** Most people tend to talk too much in interviews and oversell themselves, and they miss what the interviewer is interested in hearing. Listening cues you into what the interviewer is interested in. I've witnessed an odd phenomenon over the years: most interviewers like to talk. If they do most of the talking, it is amazing how often they will think you are brilliant. By the way, you can always stimulate interviewers to talk by simply asking questions: What are your biggest needs? How will you be evaluating the role?

Above all, be yourself. You want to connect with the interviewer. . . . Most decisions are made based on chemistry. If the chemistry is good, you will leap to the top of the heap, and anything missing from your background will become unimportant. If the chemistry is not good, then the perfect resume won't matter. Plus, you want them to hire you for who you are. You want the fit to be good as much as they want the fit to be good.

Follow up. Write a thank-you note (or a thank-you e-mail). Most people don't, and doing so will make you more impressive to the interviewer. They'll like you and remember you.

Be persistent. Don't assume that because you didn't get a job they don't like you. You may be the right person, but there is not an opportunity for you at the present time. Persistence keeps you top-of-mind when the right opportunity comes around. Just be sensitive to the fact that there is a difference between persistence and obnoxious.

Be patient—particularly in this environment. Don't look desperate—you will be less attractive as a candidate; worse, as tainted goods. One option is to consider offering your services on a consulting basis; present it as a potential win-win: The company can test-drive you without committing to a full-time hire, and you can likewise check out the fit. You are positioning yourself as someone with functional expertise they can use, not someone desperate for a job. If you have done a good job of understanding what you are good at (as described above), you will know the strengths you can leverage in this regard.

Don't lose heart. Remember what tomorrow is: A brand new day!

For example, what if, instead of talking about how you are an "excellent communicator and motivator" (lifted from a real resume that recently crossed my desk), write that you have "a strong record of turning average teams into model performers without increased pay or bonuses." That's compelling. That's someone I want to meet!

Training

Training programs for learning new professions may be a rising trend. In an interview with the *New Jersey News*, David Finegold, dean of the School of Management and Relations at Rutgers University, has called for the expansion of a national skills strategy to ensure that all U.S. job-seekers, throughout their lives, get basic skills and retraining when they decide to change careers or lose their jobs.

"The way I hope it will work is to have good support in place, have people go to post-high-school education or training or apprenticeships that could lead to a good-paying job that doesn't require a college degree," he said. "The other part of the strategy is retraining. It used to be: you got people through high school and college and into a job, and the market took care of the rest. Now more and more people have to retrain. We need a system that can cope with the specialized needs of certain sectors, so it works for folks whether it's for that entry-level job or that graduate-level job. People will have an average of six or seven significant career changes. Part of it is that people are living longer. The traditional notion that people will retire at 65 isn't true anymore. People are looking to do different things, and they're looking to do different things at different points during their lives. We need a system that will help people make those transitions."

There are several ways to gain the experience and training you need for breaking into new fields of work. Volunteering for nonprofit organizations in your area of interest or doing pro bono work can provide experience and lead to connections for a paid position. Apprentices receive paid, on-the-job learning and academic instruction that equip them with the portable skill sets needed to advance in their chosen field.

Free and low-cost resources also are available nationwide for individuals at all skill levels. The following are some sites worth checking out.

Government Programs

Career One Stop (CareerOneStop.org), and the U.S. Department of Labor (DOL.gov) focuses on job searching, resume writing, and access to phones, faxes, computers to assist with your search, as well as access to onsite and online skills development workshops and training programs, most of which are free. Features on the site include: exploring careers, education and training, finding schools, wage and salary information, benefits, job search features, and services in your area.

Temporary Agencies

Many temp agencies offer access to free tutorials designed to improve the skill level of candidates when they register. For example, a downsized accountant can sign up with Robert Half International (RHI.com), which specializes in placing accounting and finance professionals and has access to 8,000 online tutorials that cover everything from technical accounting skills to leadership and public speaking.

Learn It for Free

Open Courseware (OCW.MIT.edu) is another great educational tool that can help you learn new skills and get you excited about taking those abilities and applying them to a new job. Now with rising unemployment and more time on the hands of many, universities and colleges are posting course materials—including syllabi, class notes, and lectures—online for anyone to access. This movement, known as open courseware, allows self-learners to save money on tuition. More than 200 colleges and universities now offer courses ranging from art history to economics for free on demand. The classes can be watched on YouTube or downloaded to iPods. Education isn't just about job/career prep; it's about the human spirit that is both intelligent and curious. You won't earn a degree at OCW but you will earn the knowledge which you can apply toward a new job. Check it out, buy a school lunch box, and sign up for a class. It beats watching MTV all day.

Keep an Open Mind for New Perspectives

Be open to change. Create a list with as many areas where your skill and passion can be applied. For example, if you're a photographer, try to think of everything that needs to be photographed beyond the obvious. Justin, a wedding photographer who broke away from the competition by specializing in hilarious poses and gag photos of the wedding party made his business even more successful by taking nontraditional wedding photos that included food, pregnant bride bellies, and church mishaps.

Never limit your possibilities; jobs are always in a state of flux. New opportunities may involve taking a continuing education course at a community college, networking outside your industry, or checking out several different sections of the want ads to see what jobs might be a fit. Be ready for a challenge. You might have to learn a new lingo, have lunch with strangers, and think outside the box. Dare to live your passion. The possibilities truly are unlimited.

Overcoming Resistance

When you think about reinventing yourself, do you have a sudden burning desire to paint the bathroom or pick the lint off your sweat suit? Well, that's procrastination, a form of resistance to change. When you're excited about changing your life in theory but find yourself still doing the same old thing, have a go at these exercises to help break your patterns. Try this:

1. *Throw out some of your unnecessary junk.* According to psychologists, you might see clutter as a sign of uncertainty. Accumulating "stuff" may be preventing you from committing to a new path. Unfinished projects lying around can make it hard to focus on what's really important such as finding a course in accounting or green building certification—courses that will improve your odds for acquiring that new dream job.

2. *Start small.* Thinking of your overall goal can be overwhelming. Manage your resistance by selecting one small part and attack it today. For example, if you want to break into a certain career or business, take a small component of it, such as "skills I need," then research courses, schools, internships, or career training that will help you become better qualified.

Procrastination also arises from a fear of the unknown and a fear of change. If you use all the information and resources available, it's possible to stop fearing change, move forward, and open your mind to new ideas.

At this point, are you thinking it's time to clean out the car? Do you feel an overwhelming urge to learn how to make homemade spaghetti sauce? Wait! Maybe it's a perfect time to start growing tomatoes. Your sauce will be good enough for the Godfather, and now you've created a new business path.

Staying Afloat:
FINANCE YOUR NEW LIFE

"I've got all the money I'll ever need if I die by four o'clock this afternoon."

—*Henny Youngman*

When you go free-falling into the zero-income zone, bolster those nerves with survival strategies. Yes, there are times when reality is very scary, but have you stepped outside lately? Everyone is dealing with it on some level. It is what it is; seriously, *stop worrying about the economy and start living your life!* When you're afraid and stressed out, you might accidentally take it out on people who care about you. Instead of obsessing about your lack of income, focus on your commitment. Are you willing to do whatever it takes to stay afloat and come through on top? Good. Go and get some fear management advice from your healthcare provider, spiritual leader, or school counselor, if you need to, and then read this chapter for tips to help you stay financially afloat while you're between jobs. If you're thinking of starting your own business, you'll need a way to find start-up money. How will you do that without a job? Unfortunately, times are tough, and you're not the only one sweating it out. Banks and other lenders are more cautious about lending money, and at the end of the day they want to be paid back— surprise!—but there still are ways you can get the money to come in.

So, let's get to work! First, take an honest look at your expenses. Imagine that, no matter what happens, you'll be okay. Add up how much it costs every month to live the way you live. Chances are, your income doesn't match your lifestyle. Join the club. You may have to make some sacrifices like cutting out the manicures and lattes and make radical changes such as buying your wine in a box instead of a bottle to give yourself some room to breathe.

Do What You Have to Do!

Andy, a 42-year-old landscaper, was out of work for more than a year and intentionally became homeless. He profited from the experience and ended up with $15,000 in the bank. Here's what Andy told us:

"People say the most important thing is keeping a roof over your head, but I live in San Diego and housing is exorbitant. So the first thing to go was that huge expense: my condo. I couldn't sell it, and if I did, I'd lose money on it. So I rented it out furnished to a research scientist from the U.K. who was here on a work assignment at a local university lab. I charged him double the amount of my mortgage payment. In the process of trying to rent my house, I learned that a lot of people who were in town on extended business trips preferred to rent furnished homes.

"Before my renter moved in, I took an honest look at all the crap I owned and sold what I didn't need on Craigslist. I sold all the possessions I could live without and ended up with $2,500. I used some of the money to pay rent for a year on a small storage locker, then stashed everything else, like photo albums and sentimental things that can't be replaced, in storage. I packed a laptop, my cell phone, and suitcase with the bare minimum—seven days' worth of clothes. I moved into my Ford Explorer. For the next nine months I lived in my car. I took my showers at the gym every morning, and at bedtime I parked on a variety of safe streets near the beach, and wherever I could enjoy nature. I parked wherever it was legal and never stayed in the same spot.

"I applied and received a student loan and enrolled in a green engineering program that focused on water conservation. My rent profit covered the car payment, insurance, gas, and food, and I stashed any extra I had in the bank. I listed my service on all the free sites I could find and began getting freelance work for odd jobs like painting, hauling junk, and gardening. I saved everything I earned and realized that money adds up fast when you don't have to pay for exorbitant housing. I lived in my car until I had $15,000 saved in the bank; then I moved back into my condo. Being homeless isn't horrible when you don't have a family or a lot of responsibilities. I'm in the best shape of my life because I went to the gym every day, and I spent a lot of time at the beach reading and studying. I experienced some amazing sunrises, met new people, and hung out in a lot of coffee shops. I made new friends, and I met a really great woman I'm dating now, all because I lost my job and had to make some drastic choices. When I finished school, I was hired right out of my training program by a water conservation company. It worked out, and I am a better person for it."

> "I saved everything I earned and realized that money adds up fast when you don't have to pay for exorbitant housing. I lived in my car until I had $15,000 saved in the bank; then I moved back into my condo."

Homelessness isn't for everyone, but scaling back on expenses is your first line of defense. If "you are what you think" is true, then dismiss all your beliefs that you're poor. Replace "I don't have money" with "I have money coming to me." Then use that surge of energy you get from psyching yourself up to fill out grant and loan applications as well as proposals for venture capital. And buy one of those battery-powered gadgets that counts your loose change and drops it into quarter, nickel, and dime rolls, because that, my friend, is the wave of the future!

So how can you cut your overhead and buy some time to get back on your feet while you're searching for a new job or launching a business? If you have a family and can't leave your house, consider moving everyone into the biggest bedroom and renting your spare bedrooms to foreign exchange students. Agencies will pay as much as $600 per month for a college student to live in your home. If you host a couple, you'll get double the money. In most cases, you have to serve one meal a day to them as part of the program. Kids camping out in your bedroom might get on your nerves, and you'll have to get creative when you need some privacy, but think of the experience as an opportunity to bond with your family on a level you've never experienced before and learn the art of communal cohabitation and another language. (Other cultures have mastered this, but Americans have a lot to learn.) You can learn patience, tolerance, teamwork, generosity, and organization skills all while learning about other cultures. If you're single, team up with other people who need a friend or help running their house, like single parents, divorced people, parents, grandparents, or an elderly person who shouldn't live alone. In exchange for rent, you can give them emotional support, listen to their problems, and cheer them up. You can run errands for them or help with housekeeping and maintenance. Teaming up is sometimes better for the whole community than going it alone.

Another way to consolidate is to roll your social life into networking meetings. Instead of spending money on dinners and movies, go to business mixers. Meet people, get their card, and follow up with them. Keep in touch and form alliances. They might refer you to someone who will hire you, or if you're starting a business, they might refer you to clients or become your clients. To find business networking groups in your area, visit Meetup.com.

Ways to Float Through Life When You're Not Making Money

- Move in with your grandparents. Drive them around and run errands for them in exchange for free rent.
- Live in your car or camp in a friend's driveway.
- Travel around the world and couch-surf for free; visit CouchSurfing.com for details.
- Fill your house with foreign exchange college students.
- Rent your home and move into a small apartment in a less desirable neighborhood.
- Barter with newly divorced people; in exchange for free rent, offer emotional support or to help them run their house.

Unemployment and Other Income

If you're entitled to unemployment benefits, be sure to file a claim by calling your state labor department. You'll need to stay on the case and make sure your employer pays you promptly for the time you worked, any severance pay they promised, and—if your state mandates it — any unused vacation time. You can find out how to apply for unemployment benefits in your state on CareerOneStop.org, a site funded by the U.S. Department of Labor.

If you contributed to an employer-sponsored retirement savings account like a 401(k), learn how to access that money to roll it over into your own account, but don't cash it out unless you're in dire straits (living in your car doesn't count). Don't forget: tax penalties come with cashing out. If you can swing it and won't be working for a while or will be starting your own business, you'll want to try your best to sock away at least *something*—maybe that latte or manicure money—for retirement.

Feeling Clueless About Unemployment Benefits?

Consider your cluelessness an accomplishment. You've never before had to find out if you qualify for unemployment benefits until now. At Help WithUnemployment.com, you can download their free guide to applying for unemployment benefits. The guide offers help for both first-time filers and those with previous experience. There, you'll find tips and resources on these topics:

- The best and easiest ways to file
- How to maintain your unemployment benefits
- How long you can stay on unemployment
- Where to find jobs that are right for you

Loans, Angel Money, and Venture Capital

The world of finance might look bleak when you watch the news but, according to the National Venture Capital Association, there are a slew of investors out there looking for bright ideas to finance. Loans and grants for start-ups also are available, if you can prove you have a viable plan and something to leverage against a loan. Visit Start Up Weekend (StartupWeekend.com) to find out how to meet investors and business partners. Investors love to find the next big thing, so if you have a product, software, Web site, or service with huge potential, check this out. There's a difference between venture capitalist (VC) firms and angel investors. If you're trying to raise less than $1 million, you need an angel investor, not a venture capitalist. A VC firm prefers to fund businesses with the potential to be enormous. Angels, of course, are looking for a huge hit, but they're much more willing to fund smaller companies that will require less capital. Angel funders haven't shut down. There are still plenty of wealthy individuals who want to fund small start-ups. Sources of angel investing also can include friends and family. You often can find a local angel investor, membership organization, or club that networks and shares investment leads.

Where to Go to Look for Start-up Dough

Angel Capital Association (AngelCapital.org), Go for Funding (Go ForFunding.com), AngelInvestorNetwork.com, and the AngelInvestor Directory.com are some great sites for garnering funds for your start-up. They're all different, but the end result is the same: you get cash for your brilliant idea. Some may charge fees for making presentations, and some may charge a fee to apply for consideration, but it's a legitimate way to go. The best way to find angel investors is to network with business leaders, wealthy individuals, and professionals such as accountants, lawyers, or financial advisors. A word of advice: try to approach angels who are less than two degrees of separation from you so they will already have sound knowledge of your background and character. You should ask everybody you know, not whether they want to invest, but whether they know anybody who might want to make an investment in you and your great idea.

Tough times weed out weak competition. If your business has staying power, don't be surprised if you find yourself succeeding. If you can hang on through the lean (or lien, some may call it) time, you'll be in the ideal position to prosper when the economy recovers.

If you're a bootstrap entrepreneur, chances are you'll be starting businesses in the field where you formerly worked full time in order to leverage your experience and network of contacts.

For example, Terri worked as a television meteorologist in Charlotte, North Carolina, for 17 years. She was at the top of her game, widely respected and already had received prestigious awards when she was let go. Terri said, "They would hold me to my noncompete clause so I couldn't work in Charlotte in a similar job for another year." But Terri did find a way to work in the same field, raise some seed money, and start her own business venture. "Lucky for me, my husband and I discovered a nice little hole in that noncompete and we launched TerriBennett.com in Charlotte." The Web site was quite rudimentary at first but it allowed Terri to continue doing what she loved: forecasting the weather, offering backyard astronomy tips, and answering weather questions in a daily column. She learned how to shoot, edit, and crunch video for the Internet and added a video blog to the site. She and the hubby had a set built, with cameras, lights, and audio equipment and proceeded to offer a daily video blog with weather and astronomy information. Along the way she started adding simple environmental messages to show people how easy it was to do their part to lead less wasteful and more sustainable lifestyles. "We decided to call it 'Do Your Part,' and we launched DoYourPart.com," she said. "We have a family of sponsors behind us, and the future is bright!"

"So yes, I say it loud and clear," she states happily: "Thank you for firing me!"

None of this would have happened had Terri not lost her job or been married to such a smart guy. "So yes, I say it loud and clear," she states happily: "Thank you for firing me!"

Microlenders

Microlenders often are nonprofit organizations that make small business loans to people who would not ordinarily qualify for a bank loan. The microfinance concept started in developing countries about 30 years ago and came to the United States in the early 1990s. Lately this resource has received a boost from federal lawmakers. They added substantial new financing for microloans to the economic stimulus package approved in 2009. Here's great news for start-ups—they allocated $30 million to the Small Business Administration's microloan program, which was added to the agency's existing $20 million earmarked for microloans.

The Small Business Administration's microloan program provides small loans ranging from under $500 to $35,000. Under this program, the SBA makes funds available to nonprofit intermediaries that, in turn, make the loans directly to entrepreneurs, including veterans. Funds can be used for typical business needs including working capital, machinery and equipment, inventory, and leasehold improvements. Interest rates are negotiated between the borrower and the intermediary.

Lenders like Accion Network at Accion.org, help the little guy/gal. They lend to all sorts of entrepreneurs, including caterers, florists, hair salons, day-care centers, even online publishers. First-time loans range from $500 to $25,000, with terms of up to 60 months, filling a void for start-ups that may not have access to traditional bank credit. You will have to submit a business plan with your application, but you should already have that in the works. Accion charges an annual interest rate of 12 to 16 percent on its loans (plus a 5 percent origination fee) and tries to help its clients qualify for traditional bank financing after building their businesses and credit track records. Are you a solid person who has integrity and commitment but your credit isn't what it used to be? Then microlenders might be for you. They don't judge you by your credit score. They look at your character and business experience.

Credit Unions

Credit unions still have money to lend! Unlike large banks, credit unions make loans primarily using deposited funds from their members. Credit unions have an edge over many banks; they boast competitive interest rates, a required credit score of just 640, and closing fees that they say are hundreds of dollars below many banks. To combat their reputation as too inconvenient to be a good alternative to traditional banks, credit unions have opened branches in grocery stores and launched online services. Some have created networks that allow customers—or "members" as the industry calls them—to use one another's branches. Many credit unions are now open to the public, no longer limiting service to employees at a particular company or industry. Sometimes you just have to live in the state; other times you need to belong to an organization. Credit unions are originating a lot more business loans than they have in the past because many banks have gone belly up. So credit unions, like microlenders, are a relatively small source of small business lending, but with many banks in bad shape, they may be increasingly important in the years ahead.

Bad Times for Banks, Good Times for Credit Unions

According to the Credit Union National Association (CUNA), credit unions are for everyone, but the law places some limits on the people they may serve. A credit union's charter defines its "field of membership," which could be an employer, church, school, or community. Anyone working for an employer that sponsors a credit union, for example, is eligible to join that credit union.

If you don't belong, CUNA offers these tips on how to find a credit union to join:

1. *Call CUNA.* The Credit Union National Association—CUNA.org—can help you find a credit union. By calling (800) 358-5710, you'll hear an electronic message that includes the name and telephone number of a person at the credit union league in your state who can help you find a credit union to join.
2. *Call your state league.* A representative will tell you about credit unions in your area that you are eligible to join.
3. *Ask your boss.* If you're still employed, your company may sponsor a credit union or may be a select employee group (SEG) that has access to a credit union. Many employers offer direct deposit of payroll to your credit union.
4. *Poll your family.* Does your spouse's employer sponsor a credit union? Most credit unions allow credit union members' families to join. Each credit union, however, may define "family" differently. At some, only members of your immediate family are eligible. At other credit unions, family may include extended family members, such as cousins, uncles, and aunts.
5. *Quiz the neighbors.* Some credit unions have a "community" field of membership, serving a region defined by geography rather than by employment or some other association. Ask friends in the community if they know of a credit union you may join.

Both these nonprofit lending sectors are experiencing growth. Entrepreneurs should consider whether they can meet their financing needs through a credit union or microlender before turning to potentially high-cost options like credit cards, loan sharks, or the mob.

Like banks, credit unions offer checking and savings accounts, car loans, and home mortgages. Deposits are guaranteed up to $250,000, just as at banks.

"Most credit unions have plenty of liquidity and have for years made prudent loans at very competitive rates and terms, and we're not about to stop now," John Reed, president/CEO of Maine Savings FCU, told us. "The fallout from delinquent home loans and subprime lending has caused many banks to hold onto their cash and lend much more conservatively than they had been. More people are turning to credit unions for loans they might have gone to a bank for a year or two ago."

Brother Can You Spare a Loan?

Peer-to-peer lending is an industry that allows consumers to participate as either a borrower or a lender. Organizations such as VirginMoney .com, Zopa.com, LendingClub.com, Prosper.com, and PertuityDirect .com compete with each other to make loans, often resulting in lower rates for borrowers than are available on unsecured bank loans. To use the services, borrowers typically sign up on the Web site and provide a credit history on which their interest rate is based. Those in need of money post their specs—for example, $3,000 to consolidate credit card debt or $9,000 to expand a small company—and lenders bid for the business. It is all done anonymously, and borrowers are not inundated with e-mails and telephone calls as are borrowers registering with traditional online lending companies. Borrowers must have an established credit record and must meet the sites' minimum credit score and debt-to-income ratio thresholds. These Web sites work great for relatively small, unsecured, and primarily personal loans. Peer-to-peer lending is all about people helping people. Wow, what a great concept!

So Many Grants, So Little Time

Grant money might not be as abundant as in the old days (like 2007), but there are resources. Check out SCORE.org, a nonprofit association of executives who counsel small business owners—for free. Another resource for entrepreneurs is the Small Business Administration's Small Business Development Centers. Each state has a Governor's Office of Economic Development, which helps fund classes, workshops, and other services at the centers. Search for your state governor in your favorite search engine, and visit SBA.gov for a list of grants for which you can apply. More sources for borrowing and raising money are listed in the back of this book. But a word of warning: there are lots of grant scams out there, so look for some sort of seal of approval, and double-check that source as well. There is no forest of money trees growing in some guy's backyard, so don't believe everything you hear.

While you're investigating these endless possibilities, enjoy the wonders of everything that's free: air, sunsets, love, and a free dessert on your birthday. Advice is also usually free, but most of the time it isn't worth half that much. Use your intuition and go with what feels right. You'll make it! We know you will. And whatever you do—if you end up losing everything—hang onto this book!

CHAPTER SIX

Your Support Network:
DON'T BAIL OUT!

*"By working faithfully eight hours a day, you may eventually
get to be a boss and work 12 hours a day."*

—Robert Frost

You're not alone on this unemployed, need a new job/career/lifestyle/ business adventure. But, when it's all said and done, we're sitting here in our nice living room or hot bathtub and you are out there . . . alone. That makes us kind of sad. No one should try and start something as enormous as reinventing themselves all by themselves, so we're going to get you some real live assistance. Not the blow-up doll kind, but humans who can help you create, delegate, and put a team together to help you achieve your dreams.

First off, we hope that somewhere inside of yourself you have a fantastic idea for a creative work-at-home job, a new business, or a freelance career. Maybe you're still percolating the idea, but you want to toss the idea back and forth with someone. You need someone else to connect with. The poet John Donne sagely wrote "No man is an island," and it's true. You need backup. You know, like Batman had Robin. Wonder Woman had her sidekick, Wondergirl, and Superman had a weird relationship with Jimmy in the newsroom. Have you checked out the cover of this book? There are two authors, not one. We figured it out and so can you.

In this chapter you'll find sites, ideas, professional advice, and personal stories of successful people who reached out for a little help. No ego bruising involved. Read on and find out who or what we suggest you have as your wingman in this new journey.

Megan's father was a CEO at a large company and always taught his daughter that if she wanted to be a success she needed a support network. Here is her story:

"After I was laid off from my job at a big marketing firm the first person I called was my dad. He offered me some guidance, $500, and a few contacts, but he told me that I needed to bring a personal board of directors into my life if I was really serious about a career. He said I needed mentors not only to help me in my job search but [also] to help me with my finances and relationships. My friends got on board with my makeover and challenged me to step outside my comfort zone in order to pursue what I really want to do, which was to enter public relations where I could write and be more creative. They also encouraged me to dump my loser boyfriend, but that's another story. I next went to see a life coach to help define my goals. He encouraged me to go back to school to get my MBA. Between my friends and my life coach and my dad, I feel more in tune with my decisions about my career and my life. I now have two job offers in this crazy economy, and I don't think I could have done it without my family, my friends, or my coach."

If you're afraid of losing your job or savings or the ax has already fallen, you're bound to be freaking out. That's natural. Worrying is our way of being in tune to anything that threatens our safety or well-being. Write down your concerns if you can't sleep. Then take some time to think over your list. Call up some friends and talk over your concerns with them. Odds are you will find they are also worried about the same issues, and you can form a sort of community to work out your problems. If you catch yourself obsessing about the same things over and over again, stop and focus on the task at hand. If you've been laid off or fired, realize that you're not alone. Don't let these feelings prevent you from calling others for support. Make sure that no matter how bad the work or financial situation, you can ask for help. You may find this really hard to do. Maybe you're too proud or you're afraid to ask for favors, or maybe you just don't know whom to talk to. But honestly, in this global economic meltdown, we're all in it together. Network with other people, as suggested earlier. Check with professionals when you feel stumped, whether it's for career advice or emotional help. City, county, state, and federal resources are listed on the Internet as well as your local psychological association and mental health and credit counseling agencies. You really do need someone to talk to besides the dog. If you're really feeling desperate, put down the book and dial 911. Take care of yourself, because even though we've never met, we care.

Reasons to Ask for Help

- *Experience*—You may find people who are experts at the new career you have chosen. If you can find a mentor or hire a professional, you could be assured of making the right moves from the very beginning.
- *No Worries*—A professional can identify the issues that can cause your business problems from the get-go. If you ask for help in the very beginning, you can nip potential crises in the bud.
- *Relationship Matters*—Consultants may have contacts with the press, potential clients, or CEOs of companies you may want to pitch to and can be very helpful in the long run.
- *You'll Keep Learning*—By hooking up with a consultant or someone who has been around the proverbial block a few times, you'll acquire knowledge that you can apply again and again. Once you learn and understand, you, yourself, will become the expert.

The Association of Solopreneurs (we think they made that word up, but that's cool)—Solopreneurs.org—and the people behind it, provide training and coaching that allows you to learn the best practices and make informed decisions about your business. For a fee, you can join this group and have access to all sorts of things such as grants and teleclasses, and, when things really get rough, you can call experts and talk to them on their hotline. It beats calling some other hotlines that the perpetually lonely tend to dial, right?

Linda Sager is a pioneer in Hollywood; she's a female script consultant for clients such as TriStar Pictures, Ray Bradbury, Tony Bill, and production companies and writers from six continents, but she didn't do it alone. Here is her story:

"I entered the film and television industry 30 years ago, when there were few women. I began my own business as a script consultant, partly because I realized that a woman over 25 would have trouble making it in Hollywood. I also realized that unless someone had a male mentor, finding a job and moving up the corporate ladder probably wouldn't happen. I had to figure out how to get mentored and how to get a team around me to help in all those areas I didn't know. I knew drama well, but didn't know marketing, or resume writing, or administration, or how to create a business. I realized I had to form my own team and create my own mentors and consultants. I found a brilliant career consultant who began to help me work out a team. I found a publicist when my first book was ready to come out who also helped me with marketing. Next I found a media consultant, a financial consultant for when I began to do well, a clothes consultant, a time-management consultant, and a seminar consultant. There were two qualities I looked for: the consultant had to be good at what she/he did and had to be supportive of my goals. Since I had very little money, sometimes I did trades with other consultants, but other times I simply saved my money. If I could only afford 30 minutes a month with the person, then I did that. I also explored this other way of thinking, and I began nurturing other women's careers, even careers that were competitive with mine. I soon became interested in studying about women, women's roles, and women's management styles. I received a master's degree in feminist theology all because I wasn't afraid to ask for help."

> *"I began my own business as a script consultant, partly because I realized that a woman over 25 would have trouble making it in Hollywood."*

As soon as others begin sharing their ideas and thoughts with you, you can start to grow your business or new career. And you need those folks because, after all, you can't expect to be us—experts at everything. But we want you to keep moving forward. If the advice of one or two people is good, then how about hearing from hundreds of other people at Web 2.0? This site offers collaboration and brainstorming with all types of people in lots of different businesses. Better yet, you can dig deeper within Mindjet.com, BrainReactions.com, MindMeister.com, and other such sites to come up with a brilliant plan to take over the world—or at least to get your cookie business off the ground. You also can tap into the latest trends for your new project that's sure to bring in cash with sites like IconCulture.com and TrendWatching.com.

HAL 9000 or Virtual Assistant?

You may have innovative ideas and business plans but you need extra help . . . like a gal Friday, or a robot, or *someone*, for the love of God, who can help with all the paperwork and filing as you find yourself drowning in the details. Not to worry, we have the answer: you need to outsource your tasks to a virtual assistant.

What to Expect from Your Virtual Assistant

Your virtual assistant (VA) works from home or an outside office that you don't pay for. VAs specialize in everything from accounting to word processing and Web design to administration, writing, and editing.

They can help you prepare reports, transcribe audio, edit manuals, and translate documents. It's also their job to manage your appointment scheduling, CRM (customer relationship management), updates, blog posts, and shopping cart. Add to that airline and hotel reservations, travel arrangements, and event planning. Also they deal with customer service support, including returning phone calls and e-mail; teleseminar and Webinar announcements; bookkeeping; vendor management; and personal shopping. All this happens without office drama, because your VA isn't in your office.

Just a hint: if you're looking for a cool job, maybe *you* can become a virtual assistant like Stacy. She says:

"I was fired from what was to become the last 'real' job I ever had. I worked as a travel consultant at the time and was also the IT person for the agency. I'd been asked by the vice president who happened to be the husband of the owner, to load a game for him on our computer system. Our VP liked to play when in the office, so I did what I was told. A couple of weeks later, the president of the company fired me for installing the game. I was stunned! I remember feeling intensely that I never wanted to be in a position where a boss could pull the rug out from under me again. Within weeks, I'd started working for myself scheduling travel for my old clients, but from my home. This continued for years until I started to wonder if there was something more for me out there, and I started looking around. I found Coach University and felt drawn to coaching. One day, the president of Coach University put out an e-mail blast announcing that the founder of the company had decided to go on sabbatical for two years, traveling North America in his RV, and wanted someone to run his life. I raised my virtual hand; we talked and started working together. I became his virtual assistant at my home in Baltimore, while he roamed the country in his RV.

"Because of his high media profile at that time, a journalist approached me to do a piece about my virtual assistance work. When that piece ran, hundreds of women came out of the woodwork wanting me to tell them how I did my job.

"Seeing an opportunity, I founded my company, Assist, to train, coach, support, certify, and refer truly extraordinary virtual assistants. In doing so, I formalized an entirely new profession, which has become quite a big deal with thousands and thousands of virtual assistants worldwide, and several VA organizations on several continents.

> *"If that woman hadn't fired me, I'd probably still be an hourly wage earner, doing the nine-to-five in an office, impacting no one and nothing."*

"I am delighted beyond measure to do what I do today helping people—usually former administrative assistants beaten down by the corporate world—build solid businesses that contribute to their having high-quality lives.

"If that woman hadn't fired me, I'd probably still be an hourly wage earner, doing the nine-to-five in an office, impacting no one and nothing. Instead, I was able to discover what I was really made of, who I really am, and live a life I adore."

Hiring People Just Like You

If you feel the need to hire a real, live person whom you can interact with face to face, consider an independent contractor. Someone who is kind of like you: freelancer, independent consultant (IC), or entrepreneur. Sound familiar? The cool thing is you can pick that person's brain, and because many employment laws and tax rules that cover employees don't apply to ICs, you can save time and money by hiring ICs instead of employees. ICs provide a level of flexibility that you can't get with "real" employees. You can pay an IC to accomplish only a specific task, allowing your business to get specialized expertise for a short period—without having to pay for training. That's all well and good, but there is one tiny caveat. When you hire an IC to create something like a computer program, written work, artwork, musical work, or anything in the multimedia arena, you need to be concerned about copyright ownership.

The copyright laws contain a major trap for unwary bosses such as you. You won't own the copyright to the IC's work unless you obtain a written assignment of copyright ownership or a work-for-hire agreement. An assignment is simply a transfer of copyright ownership. You should obtain an assignment before the IC starts work. This assignment should be included in the IC agreement, and if we haven't suggested it before, make an attorney one of your best friends.

But don't burn out on all work and no fun. A successful life is a balanced life. Grab some friends and have a "Thank You For Firing Me!" party. Take advantage of the downtime to get close to your friends and neighbors. If you don't have friends (which sometimes happens when you go broke), go to networking meet-ups and invite some people over (BYOB or potluck). Parties are energizing!

Even if you're flying solo and working for yourself, you don't have to be by yourself. There are plenty of people who want you to succeed and who want to help you make the big bucks. You only have to ask. And what about us, you ask? We want to hear your stories. Send us an e-mail or a video if you had a particularly great party. We're posting your videos and stories (like the ones you're reading here) on ThankYouFor FiringMe .org, so no one has to feel like he or she is alone. We're not going anywhere as long as we remain on your bookshelf. We're here to stay, and we've got your back.

CHAPTER SEVEN

Your Winning Game Plan:
HOW TO ACHIEVE A LIFE YOU LOVE

"A good rule of thumb is if you've made it to 35 and your job still requires you to wear a name tag, you've made a serious vocational error."

—Dennis Miller

You're starting to feel empowered and enlightened, and you are taking charge of your life—maybe for the first time ever! You're doing the exercises we created, and you've started to map out your new career or job. How great is that? You're not floundering anymore. You're taking the tools we're offering you and creating a game plan. The universe is saying there's a new and better adventure in store for you. You're entering the future. You now have a new beginning, a new adventure, and a load of ideas to get you started. Whoopie!

Surfing for a New Career

Like we've stated before, learning to surf is very much like searching for a new career path. When you've mastered the skill of hanging ten and you find yourself angling down the wave, you'll realize you accomplished what you set out to do and life is good again.

Keep the hunt for a new career simple and uncomplicated. You're under enough stress as it is, so don't continually make lists of places to drop off your resume. Think about where you want to work or what type of work you want to do, and begin there. Make an inventory of your strengths, and build on them. Work on that for a while, and then go out and take a walk on the beach or, better yet, go surfing! The bills and the scary world will still be there when you come home, but now you'll be relaxed and able to get a firm grip on reality without freaking out. Now that you have the stress under control, take it up a notch and seek some advice from people who have actual jobs or are consultants. Invite them to lunch and pitch ideas or slide them your resume when you reach for dessert. It's that simple. People are more than willing to help in this nutty economy, and so you need to be able to accept their council and offers with grace. If you don't know what your strengths are, *ask*. The people who know you will tell you what they are. People love to feel like they're contributing—be sure to thank them and appreciate their contribution.

Catch a Wave

Friends, family, and colleagues are your most important assets. You can stare at the Internet until you go blind, and you still won't have that new life. Instead, call friends and family and share your great idea for a new business. A few years ago they might have been negative and told you to get a "real job," but in this day and age, odds are they will be supportive. Imagine your dad bragging to his buddies about your great idea to buy a Miracle-Ear franchise. Imagine your sister's excitement when you show her your plans to start designing lingerie. By now you've realized you had to make changes in your life even before you got the sack. You've got ideas galore, you've sent positive energy out into the world, and you're expecting major changes. Great. But here's the deal: remember all that free time you had, and the severance pay and the unemployment check? Well, tick tock, tick tock. It's time to put your plans into action. It's time to get back to work!

Family psychotherapist David Peters shares more expert advice with us: "We often get stuck in the vision of work as having only one career in a lifetime and being employed for years to come. This image of work is stuck because we were all raised with it. We saw it in the TV sitcoms we watched as kids. It is wired into the neural network of our brains. I mean this literally. All of our thoughts, our concepts, and our dreams are held in the brain as the activation of neural pathways—the paths that a signal takes from one brain cell to the next. When you picture your old job, you activate various neural pathways in your brain that give you the experience of thought and memory. Old habits and deeply held beliefs are networked with all our other beliefs and self-concepts. When we think of work and career, we inevitably activate the old neural pathways. But it's the old reality that no longer exists. We need to renetwork our brains to accommodate the new reality. Then we will be free to think more creatively about our work, and feel more comfortable with new career possibilities. This takes a bit of effort. If you merely read about this concept in this book, think about it for a moment, and move on—your brain will still be running with the old wiring. You can read here about the new work paradigm and think about it in a mere 10 seconds. And only the parts of your brain that read and picture work settings get affected, and only for 10 seconds. Your brain is still with the old work paradigm held in the old neural network. To rewire your brain, you have to get more active. When I'm teaching clients to change their thoughts, I teach them to work all of their brains into the change. If you read this section out loud, the part of your brain that speaks gets engaged, as does the part of your brain that listens. And the new neural network is expanded and becomes more complex. Now, if you talk about this change with a friend or family member, you do even more. The part of your brain that connects with others and teaches concepts gets wired into the new neural network. If you write down on paper this new understanding of work and career, you wire in the part of your brain that writes into the new neural network. And if you speak with more people about the new work paradigm, you expand and reinforce the new neural network even more. Get it? You want as much of your brain engaged as possible, and repeat the process often to get it fully burned in as the dominant neural network addressing your concept of work and career. Do this, and you will find much greater ease in imagining, planning, and engaging your new work and career path."

We hope the stories and advice you read about in these pages will assist you down the career path and help you find job after job for 50 years to come. We don't want you to stay in your new career for the rest of you life, now, do we? No. We want you to be happy and content, all while giving us the credit. One of the most important things we want you to get out of what you read here is never to fear being fired again.

Ride the Wave All the Way In

Kelley appreciated people, and she enjoyed teaching them. When she was fired, she realized that focusing on her weaknesses didn't work. When she started appreciating her strengths, she landed a new job and eventually created her own business. Says Kelley:

"I was fired from my midlevel management position in the restaurant industry, and I was completely shocked when it happened. I went through the stages of denial: bargaining, anger, and depression. Finally, after some serious soul searching, I was forced to think about what type of career I really wanted. I narrowed my search efforts, and several months later landed my dream job as a corporate trainer for a retail firm. I spent six years with that company, learned more about training than I had ever anticipated, and eventually launched my own business. The head office for the company that fired me is situated near the freeway, and every time I pass it, I wave and say, 'Thanks for firing me!'"

"The head office for the company that fired me is situated near the freeway, and every time I pass it, I wave and say, 'Thanks for firing me!'"

The job you find this year and a few years down the road won't give your life true meaning unless you're the reincarnation of Mother Teresa. A job is normally a way to pay the bills, put food on the table, and keep your life in balance. If this book can help you find employment that will make you happy *and* at the same time pay the bills, then you'll have life 50 percent made. At the same time, losing your job isn't something to be ashamed of because *you* are not your job! But honestly, taking control of your life and finding work that has personal relevance and meaning, no matter how big or small, short term or long term, will make you happy in the long run. The *impact* of your work is what will make a difference to you and your life. We don't think it's unrealistic to think that if we all work hard at exploring our options, happiness, meaning, and security will follow.

Everyone who picks up this book has different values. Some people want their work to give their life true meaning, damn the measly paycheck! And as we've said, we're all for it. If you can swing it, life should come before work. Coauthor Candice Reed once gave up a decent-paying sales job to write for a magazine that didn't pay much so that she could stay at home with her middle school and high school children. Paying the bills on time was a constant struggle, but helping to mold her two teens into mature, respectable, fun-loving adults without prison records was worth the sacrifice. But that might not be important to others. "Meaningful work" means different things to different people. Some people want to make a difference in the lives of others; other people just want a big, fat paycheck; and others want to be the boss. That will be your decision when you get back out into the workplace. Just remember as you're filling out those applications that there is scientific evidence that suggests that if you're unhappy at work, your home life will also be miserable. You need balance. It just doesn't make sense that you can go to a job 40 hours a week and that amount of time will not have some impact, positive or negative, on your soul. We just want to remind you of that fact before you say "yes" to the human resources director when she calls and makes an offer, because we're confident that because of our guidance and the advice of experts like John McCrea that phone call *will* come.

Angle Down the Wave Face

John McCrea, managing partner at Bialla & Associates, executive search consultants, has come up with something he calls "John's axioms," and he has offered to share this with us:

"Aptitude outweighs specific experience. I'd almost always rather hire a superstar with less specific experience than an average performer with the perfect background. He/she will achieve far more in the long run. You may have all the right stuff to be the perfect person for the job, but it may not be obvious from your resume. If you are relying on your resume to sell you, you will fail 9 times out of 10. You have no control over the way your resume is perceived. The most important thing, then, is not to get your resume in front of someone, but to get *yourself* in front of someone. The most important thing is to get a meeting. That's where you can get someone to look beyond your resume. With that in mind:

"Don't expect diddley-squat from the job boards. Job boards typically are a black hole. I deal with a lot of companies who post a job before they hire. Invariably they are inundated with hundreds and often thousands of applicants, most of whom are not even remotely right for the job. Some poor, lower-level human resources person has to sort through all of these resumes, and most of these people are too junior to really understand how to evaluate a candidate. They are overwhelmed, and the odds are you will be lost in the shuffle. Remember, your time is valuable. Put your effort into where you will get more 'bang for your buck.' If you see a job you are interested in, try to find another way in. See if you know someone who works at the company who might be able to introduce you. Doing this immediately qualifies you above others. Write directly to the CEO or hiring manager. They may pass it down to HR, but HR will look at it more closely because it was passed down to them from an important source."

Network, Network, Network!

Networking is the single most important thing you can do with your time. Network with friends, recruiters, and friends of friends, or reach out independently to people in your area of interest. For example, if you are interested in getting involved with the "green" industry, find people with whom to network who are connected to that industry. People like to engage with those who have mutual interests, so it is usually not too hard to get a meeting or a cup of coffee with someone under this pretense. Networking does these important things:

- *It gets you out and about.* Talking to people is stimulating. It gets you involved and actively discussing yourself, your career options, and your areas of interest.
- *It helps focus you.* The very act of talking to people about your area of interest will help give you ideas about how you can best fit in to that world.
- *It helps you get better at how to present yourself.* In essence, you are practicing interviewing even if these are informal meetings. You get more comfortable talking about yourself. You learn what others are interested in. You learn how to leverage your strengths.
- *Networking begets networking.* Meeting with one person may not be the answer, but that person will introduce you

to another person, who may introduce you to someone else, and so on. (You may need to ask, "Can you suggest anyone else with whom I should talk?") You extend your network, and you extend your odds of finding a great job.

- *Timing is everything in job hunting.* The more people you are speaking with, the more likely you are to find someone who has an opportunity for you or knows someone who does, so get moving and don't forget to let us know how it works out.

Part Two

Job Searching:
Dive into Cool Careers

*"When I was young I used to think that money was
the most important thing in life. Now that I'm old,
I know it is."*

—Oscar Wilde

In Part One, you found yourself without a job, but you didn't lose yourself. So now ask yourself this question: if you were a cake, and your job was the frosting, what kind of cake would you be? (Stay with us here.) Hopefully you have a pretty good handle on who *you* are, what your passion is, and how you fit into the money-making machine of life. Now that you're ready, it's time to explore the hot new jobs of the twenty-first century, emerging markets, and career ideas in this section to see what it will take to light you up. Continue using the tools we gave you in Part One to design your life around your skills and sense of accomplishment. Even if you *don't* know what kind of cake you are yet, read this section like you're sampling frosting flavors. We'll be showing you a diverse array of career options designed to give you ideas, help you brainstorm, and excite you.

You'll find out about expanding markets such as the green industry, baby boomers, and Generation Y. We'll talk about opportunities for women and fields with a growing demand for diversity. Sometimes being fired is a cue to start your own business or become an independent contractor. You'll discover what it takes to be a freelancer and how to find and use resources to help you profit from your business. You'll learn about Internet marketing, and effective ways to boost your revenue. If you're a creative person, such as an artist, writer, musician, actor, or magician—we devote an entire chapter to art and how to sell it—you'll learn how to balance the artistic with the business aspects of your profession. And finally, if you yearn for a change of place and are looking for a new adventure in a totally different country, you'll find out about opportunities to work in other parts of the world and where to find positions and careers.

Use the following chapters to get a taste of what's happening in the job market and how others have capitalized on today's trends. So grab a highlighter, mark whatever excites you—and dive in!

CHAPTER EIGHT

Big Waves Ahead:

HOT GREEN INDUSTRIES COMING YOUR WAY!

"And Lord, we are especially thankful for nuclear power, the cleanest, safest energy source there is. Except for solar, which is just a pipe dream."

—*Homer Simpson*

Green is the new black. Green is cool, it's fashionable, and by God, it's profitable. For those who don't believe in global warming, that's fine, whatever. But, hopefully if you're out of work you will at least consider a job in the green industry, because green is here to stay.

The term "green job" to us means a job with a company that offers a product or service that allows consumers to use less energy, or a paying gig that lowers the environmental impact on the planet. Apollo Alliance, a coalition of industry, labor, and environmental groups describes green-collar jobs a little differently, as those that "pay decent wages and benefits that can support a family. It has to be part of a real career path, with upward mobility. And it needs to reduce waste and pollution and benefit the environment." Yet another definition from Van Jones, author of the best-selling book, *The Green Collar Economy: How One Solution Can Fix Our Two Biggest Problems*, and founder of Green for All, defines green-collar jobs as "good local jobs that pay well, strengthen communities, provide pathways out of poverty, and help solve our environmental problems." They're slightly different views, but what matters most to us is that you find a job. Perhaps you can catch the green wave of hot jobs and ride it as long as you can.

What exactly turns a job green? According to those in charge, any job in a green company or a green division of a company is a green job. Examples of green companies and organizations include:

- Organic foods and consumer products
- Energy conservation
- Renewable energy
- Energy-efficient building
- Recycling
- Environmental cleanup
- Socially responsible investing
- Sustainable tourism
- Nonprofit environmental advocacy

Green jobs are available for men, women, teens, college students, and baby boomers—pretty much everyone. In many cases, skills you already have can evolve from white collar or blue collar, to green collar. The green industry is a rapidly developing field that changes every day. In the resource section of this book you'll find a comprehensive list of organizations and Web sites to help find jobs and training programs.

In this chapter we'll talk about why the green industry holds so much promise for a lucrative and brighter future and how you can take advantage of this expanding field.

A Field with a Future

Try and think back to 1995 when computers were first sold to the general public. They were unwieldy monsters used for writing letters and creating spreadsheets—a sort of new-age typewriter. Then, in 1998, Bill Gates presented Windows 98 to the world. Soon the Internet's explosive growth led to dot-com industries and created huge opportunities for entrepreneurs.

Like the dot-com industry, the green economy will create a massive new set of opportunities. "A global response to climate change will spur a business revolution bigger than the Internet," said cofounder of Sun Microsystems Bill Joy Sun. Could clean tech—that is, renewable energy and energy-efficient industries—actually turn out to be bigger than the

Internet? Sure it will! Clean tech will not only be superior to the Internet in dollars earned, it will eventually affect every business and industry in the world. Yes, we know that's a bold statement. But look at the facts: in early 2008, environmental data analysts at the Worldwatch Institute assessed capital flow in the green energy sector at $100 billion, with investments in alternative energies at $66 billion in 2007. Profits, jobs, and new business opportunities are waiting for you as the massive cleanup and switch to clean energy emerges. Those are the cold, green facts.

One example: Silvana and her husband, Alan, were living in Nashville and working in marketing. They decided to move to Washington to be closer to their daughter's secondary school. They found jobs with a nonprofit charity, Soles4Souls, which collects and distributes shoes around the world . . . one pair every 17 seconds. They were working from home, as a tag team, doing sales and marketing, but they were getting mediocre results and thought they might be fired. "So we took a risk and submitted a proposal to the CEO of Soles4Souls and told him we were better suited to being out with the public, doing promotional work for them," Alan said. "Since we are recent empty nesters, we suggested they buy an RV [recreational vehicle] and have us travel around the United States for a year, meeting their corporate clients, attending large-scale community shoe drives, and donating shoes to homeless shelters. They loved the idea!" Everyone else was cutting back on public relations, but the charity decided to be different and make a push in marketing their company as they collected and distributed thousands more shoes. "We've reinvented ourselves in that we stayed with the same company, yet are doing what we love: helping others and traveling," Silvana said. Soles4Souls bought the couple a 2009 RV to use as they travel the country, encouraging people to donate their gently used shoes. This keeps shoes out of landfills and gives people in developing countries usable footwear. How green is that?

"We've reinvented ourselves in that we stayed with the same company, yet are doing what we love."

The American Solar Energy Society predicted that over the next two decades at least one in four American workers will be employed in renewable energy and energy-efficiency industries. This emerging phenomenon means that more jobs and business opportunities will be available for independent contractors, from blue-collar workers to those with a PhD. Furthermore, this line of work isn't just about making money. You can feel noble about how you earn your paycheck. Remember the whole concept of reinventing yourself? Well, here's your chance to have an extended Kumbaya moment while paying the mortgage. It's time for you to change and time for the world to change. Odds are you missed that big dot-com boom or were a victim of its bust, but you may now have an opportunity to ride the green wave all the way to success and fulfillment.

Rebrand Yourself Green

What does success in a green economy look like? It looks like Dee and Troy. They were both fired from their jobs at a large American car manufacturer in Detroit. "Car sales are down. With gas prices soaring, strangely, no one seemed to think fuel prices could be the problem," Dee said. "We were scraping by and collecting unemployment when our SUV was repossessed. Our old truck that was paid for runs on diesel fuel, but where we live, diesel costs more than gas."

To cut down on fuel expenses, the couple concocted their own biodiesel using a recipe they found on the Internet. The main ingredient was discarded cooking oil collected from a Chinese restaurant. "The restaurant owner gladly gave us his used oil, since he had to pay a fee to dispose of it," Dee said. "We used nontoxic elements to purify the oil and made biodiesel in our garage for 59 cents a gallon. We don't have a college degree between us, but we figured it out. Aside from the smell of Egg Foo Yung, the truck runs great on homemade fuel."

Word got around, and soon the couple were selling homemade biodiesel to their friends for half the cost of regular diesel. Today the enterprising couple is running a lucrative business selling alternative fuel. When they were fired, they assumed they'd be searching for other jobs. But being broke and disgusted led to new purpose and adventure.

What Color Is Your Collar?

In late 2007, the Energy Independence and Security Act was passed to incorporate the Green Jobs Act of 2007, which authorizes $125 million in green-collar job training opportunities. That's enough money to train about 30,000 workers a year for jobs in emerging "green" sectors. In some cases, the high demand for green career changers translates into a larger paycheck. According to the National Renewable Energy Lab, America's growing green economy faces a looming labor shortage. This means that jobs are there for the taking. But you need to know where to find them. That's where we come to the rescue.

In 2007, Todd started a new career in global carbon trading. This was something he'd never heard of until his sister, a chemist, suggested he look into business opportunities in the strange-sounding field. "It's called cap and trade, and it's basically emissions trading—a financial technique of capping and trading pollutants," Todd said. "Carbon trading is part of Kyoto Protocol's goal to reduce certain industrial nations' greenhouse gas emissions to below-1990 levels by 2012. The idea was that countries whose emissions fall under the emissions cap—the permitted level of carbon dioxide equivalent emissions per year—could then sell those carbon credits to countries unable to meet their own caps." If that analysis sounds like Todd is a scientist with a PhD, he's not. He never even finished college. He owned a restaurant until it caught fire. That's when he found himself without a job for the first time in two decades, and without fire insurance he couldn't rebuild without going into debt.

"The hours were long and I made a little money at the restaurant, but after 20 years it wasn't any fun and my heart wasn't in it," he said. "The fire was like a sign to find something else. I wanted to be content with my life. When I found cap and trade, I became happy. This year I expect to make over $300,000, so that actually makes me rich *and* happy."

Carbon trading is a new global investment market based on emissions trading, where companies and countries have incentives to invest in developing world projects due to the highly coveted carbon credits they receive for doing just that. It's all sounds very scientific, but if Todd can do it, so can you.

Starting a green business or changing your career to green will probably require training, career counseling, or education. We've found a plethora of resources for retraining and finding jobs, and we have them listed in this chapter as well as in the resource section of this book. Most green jobs require a level of skill above a high school diploma, but many require only technical training or on-the-job training—perfect for someone who needs a job sooner than later. Not everyone has the time, the inclination, *or* the money to go back to college, but if you do you'll have more choices.

What about the average out-of-work person laid off from a factory, a store, or an office? The jobs are out there for them—and for you. Solar panels need to be manufactured and then installed. Hybrid cars must be built to replace the gas-guzzling SUVs. And don't forget the opportunities in recycling, wind farms, and buildings that need to be retrofitted. Not only will these jobs recharge the economy, but the Earth will take notice that we finally give a damn. Imagine how your life will change if you go from a high-stress career on Wall Street to a Zen-like career of planting organic crops. And who knows? You might even live a few years longer. So let's get started and turn over a new leaf.

Green Light Means Go!

Colleges and universities are catching on and teaching green. For example, the State University of New York offers a four-year degree program in alternative and renewable energy. The program focuses on wind, solar, geothermal, fuel cell, biofuel, and other emerging technologies. Students who graduate from this program will ultimately work with architects and engineers to create viable renewable energy solutions for commercial and residential facilities. Illinois State University in Normal, Illinois, offers a four-year degree program in renewable energy. Many other universities across the nation are beginning to teach courses on design and construction of solar-powered buildings, Leadership in Energy and Environmental Design (LEED), architecture, and green construction.

Dozens of community colleges offer one-year certificates and two-year associate degrees in building and installing clean energy systems. For example, Bronx Community College in New York offers solar electric training, while San Juan College, in Farmington, New Mexico, features a program in designing and installing solar energy systems. Organizations such as ICF International, Center for Environmental Health, Environmental Risk Communications, and Impact Sciences say they hire qualified people with bachelor's degrees to work on everything from clean water projects to environmental policy work. According to university officials, starting salaries nationally range between $35,000 to $45,000 for graduates of two-year programs, and $45,000 to $60,000 and upward for graduates of four-year programs. That's not too bad considering you're doing your part to save the planet *and* earning enough cash to fill up the Prius.

Green opportunities exist for both white- and blue-collar workers, with or without college degrees. Training programs for the green energy sector are offered at WorkForceAlliance.org. Organizations like EcoEmploy.com post a running list of over 500 new jobs every two weeks. The latest training programs provide new skills for everyone from carpenters to marketing executives. A growing number of universities are adding extension programs to provide specialized training for reinventing yourself. The Texas Engineering Extension Service is just one of the hundreds of university extension programs popping up throughout the country to serve those who want to adapt their skill set to the green industry.

Once you figure out that green is your career color, narrow down where exactly you might fit in. Do you feel comfortable walking on a roof, and retrofitting a house? Do you already have a set of skills that will help you land a green type of job? Are you an administrator who wants to go green or someone who wants to start from scratch and needs some additional schooling? Attend a workshop or class to gain the specialized skills required in the green economy, and check out the workshops at Solar Energy International (SolarEnergy.org), Midwest Renewable Energy Association (The-MREA.org), U.S. Green Building Council (USGBC .org) and Solar Living Institute (SolarLiving.org). Focus on what you want first, and then find people who are doing the same job that you have your eye on. Talk to these professionals, and take their advice before sending out your resume.

Now figure out where you want to work. Do you have to move to another state or city to land the green job about which you are dreaming? Research which companies are on the forefront of the green economy, and see which types of positions they have open for someone with your skills or desires. Kick off your research by learning more about green-oriented companies and the types of jobs available there by visiting the job board at the American Solar Energy Society (ASES.org). It's one of the best and informative Web sites we've come across in our green job hunt for you.

Catch the Clean Tech Wave

Anybody who lacks the desire, the money, or the time to attend college, can find plenty of opportunities for so-called green-collar jobs. These jobs are available to workers who have a basic education and general skills. The best thing is, these jobs are stable, with wages that provide benefits and security. Opportunities such as solar installation, printing with, nontoxic inks and dyes, bike delivery services, and water retrofits that increase water efficiency and conservation are out there waiting for you. Can you fill out an application? Then do it!

Green-collar job prospects are growing. In 2007, energy-renewable and energy-efficient industries offered 8.5 million jobs in the United States. This figure could reach 40 million jobs by 2030, according to a report commissioned by the American Solar Energy Society.

Van Jones, a social activist in Oakland, California, is not only an inspiration but also an expert at matching underprivileged kids with green-collar jobs. Jones, a Yale Law School graduate, heads up the Ella Baker Center for Human Rights in Oakland, which helps youngsters avoid jail and find jobs. The way he sees it is simple: as the government requires buildings to be more energy efficient, more work will be created to retrofit buildings across America with solar panels, insulation, and other weatherizing materials. "So who will do the hard and noble work of actually building the green economy?" Jones wrote in his book, *The Green Collar Economy.* "The answer: millions of ordinary people, many of whom do not have good jobs right now. According to the National Energy Lab, the major barriers to a more rapid adoption of renewable energy and efficiency are not financial, legal, technical, or ideological. One big problem is simply that green employers can't find enough trained, green-collar workers to do all the jobs."

Jones's group and the electrical union in Oakland created the Oakland Apollo Alliance in 2008, and the coalition helped to raise

$250,000 from the city government to create a union-supported training program that will teach young people in Oakland how to install solar panels and weatherize buildings.

"If we can get these youth in on the ground floor of the solar industry now, where they can be installers today, they'll become managers in five years and owners in ten. And then they become inventors," said Jones, who also spearheaded the Clean Energy Jobs Bill. "The green economy has the power to deliver new sources of work, wealth, and health to low-income people—while honoring the Earth. If you can do that, you just wiped out a whole bunch of problems."

Plant Yourself in the Green Workforce

How does setting up a sustainable energy economy translate to hot jobs and businesses? The good news is that companies such as Sony, Continental Airlines, and Wal-Mart—some you'd least expect—are going green. Clean tech is growing in three ways:

1. *Demand*: the job of figuring out how to use natural resources more efficiently and figuring out how current technology can be changed to clean and green
2. *Supply*: creating new green technologies
3. *Development*: investing venture capital in cottage industries and partnering with newly emerging green companies

In addition to private investment groups, even giant blue-chip companies are fueling the green revolution by helping clean-tech start-up companies gain momentum. Tech giant IBM promised to commit $1 billion a year to energy efficiency. As part of IBM's "Big Green" initiative, the company's venture arm is on the lookout for the next clean tech start-ups. Large companies will help start-up companies by investing money to make sure their technology works the way it should, and then provide sales leads and introductions to customers.

Christine was laid off from a large investment bank during the recession. Like many of her colleagues on Wall Street, she found herself lost without the career she had spent so much effort building over the years. With nothing left to lose, Christine went back to what she had always loved in life—fashion and the environment. Her entrepreneurial spirit still intact, Christine decided to launch her own environmentally friendly fashion line. She became a familiar face in the New York City garment district, meeting with cut-and-sew contractors, learning from experienced designers, and taking sewing classes herself. Christine networked endlessly with socialite circles and took the time to listen to whoever could help her. The designer's hard work paid off within a year, when her labor of love—the cmarchuska store (cmarchuska.com) officially hit the fashion scene.

"I love fashion and have a strong love for the environment," she said. "So I figured out a way I could tie the two together."

As the founder and designer for cmarchuska, Christine has completed the Signature Collection, which consists of chic knit basics and dresses made from the finest organic/recycled material. All of the items are manufactured in the New York City garment district, where Christine established her creative roots. Christine's ambition is not only to provide eco-friendly, high fashion clothing but also to promote philanthropy and environmental awareness through cmarchuska. The designer also supports notable charities such as Safe Horizon by donating a percentage of net profits. The stylish top you buy is only as impressive as the message behind it, and Christine's designs definitely remind people to make a positive impact on the Earth and society.

New vehicles and transportation products made to improve the environment and save people money on fuel costs are appearing on the market and attracting buyers. Whether you invent, manufacture, or sell anything related to energy-efficient transportation, you might be surprised to find a profitable niche in this sector of the green industry.

The day Liz was fired from her customer service job at a retail chain in Florida, she put up her car for sale and test-drove an electric motorcycle. "Riding in the salty air along the coast was the perfect antidote to my crappy, underpaid job," Liz recalled. "I hated that place. I used to have to unload the supply trucks, run a cash register, and even clean the freaking restroom. I was happy to leave."

The fuel cost of her clean, quiet hog was hard to quantify. Her electric bill didn't look dramatically different after she plugged in the charger, and riding a motorcycle was a great psychological boost while she was unemployed. In fact, Liz loved the electric motorcycle so much that she set up her own online dealership. "I sell them to people all over the world from a Web site I created and maintain," she said. "The manufacturer drop-ships directly to buyers after I forward them the orders. I love my bike and I love my job. I'll never unload a truck or clean another public restroom again."

A Little More Green

The top 10 emerging green industries:

- Retrofitting buildings to increase energy efficiency
- Expanding mass transit and freight rail
- Constructing "smart" electrical grid transmission systems
- Wind power
- Solar power
- Advanced biofuels
- Hydro power
- Geothermal
- Bioenergy
- Hydrogen and fuel cells

The top 10 emerging specialized green careers:

- Sales and account management
- Planet protectors: legal careers
- Installers
- Computer-aided drafting (CAD)
- Project management
- City planning
- Information technology (IT) specialist
- Organic farming
- Geographic information system (GIS) specialists
- Ecotourism

We want to reiterate our claim that America's growing green economy faces a looming labor shortage in sectors such as manufacturing, construction, and installation. In a 2005 survey by the National Association of Manufacturers, 90 percent of respondents indicated a moderate to severe shortage of qualified, skilled production employees like machinists and technicians. As we pointed out earlier in this chapter, the National Renewable Energy Lab has identified a shortage of skills and training as a leading barrier to renewable energy and energy-efficiency growth. We're not making this stuff up. Jobs considered "green collar" include organic farmers; electricians who install solar panels; plumbers who install solar water heaters; and construction workers who build energy-efficient green buildings, wind power farms, and other clean, renewable, sustainable energy development. But that's not all. Scientists and engineers who invent, design, and test new green products are needed as well as the managers, human resources professionals, and administrative teams necessary to manage, train, and support those with green-collar jobs.

Green fever has indeed sprouted around the world, and there's no sign it will slow down anytime in the future. Of course, green isn't for everyone, nor is it your only choice for embarking on your new job adventure. We can't promise that a green job is out there waiting for you to pick it and grow, but we think if you give the idea time to ripen . . . well, you get it.

Ten Web sites with Green Job Listings and Career Training Resources

GreenJobs.com

This site features a green job directory of the latest green jobs and training from worldwide government resources and associations. They offer a resume-posting service and help with creating a resume that translates to opportunities in green industries.

Ecotourism.org

Tourism is the largest business sector in the world economy, and ecotourism is growing at three times the rate of the tourism sector itself. This site offers a range of jobs that support green travel. These employees generally work for private companies, government and public institutions, and nonprofits.

Planning.org

The American Planning Association works with local governments addressing the challenges of how they can reduce a community's carbon footprint. Governments are turning to city planning professionals for direction. Opportunities exist in fields such as wetlands restoration, storm water management, transportation, and urban design.

ApolloAlliance.org

The Apollo Alliance is a coalition of business, labor, environmental, and community leaders working to catalyze a clean energy revolution in America to reduce our nation's dependence on foreign oil, cut the carbon emissions that are destabilizing our climate, and expand opportunities for American businesses and workers. The Apollo Alliance promotes policies to put millions of Americans to work in a new generation of well-paid, green-collar jobs, and make America a global leader in clean energy products and services.

Earthjustice.org

When government agencies or private interests violate (or fail to enforce) our nation's environmental laws, Earthjustice attorneys—who represent citizen groups, scientists, and other interested parties—go to court to ensure that our laws are obeyed and enforced. Job and training listings include nationwide positions for attorneys, clerks, press secretaries, internships, externships, clerkships, and more.

Eco-ventures.org

EVI runs green enterprise development projects, provides direct training and training-of-trainer programs, facilitates market linkage and value chain development, manages learning networks and dialogues, and develops training curricula and other environmental enterprise learning tools. EVI research and programs include environmental enterprises related to renewable energy, water, agriculture, organics, nontimber forest products, recycling, natural fibers, and alternative fuels.

USGBC.org

The U.S. Green Building Council is dedicated to education, training, and employment placement in green construction. Their career center page helps connect members with new employment opportunities. The page features links for job seekers, employers, and recruiters to access their specialized niche. Job seekers can post resumes, create job alerts, and view jobs. Employers and recruiters can post jobs and view resumes.

SVN.org

Social Venture Network (SVN) transforms how the world does business by leveraging its members' collective strengths of leadership, knowledge, and enterprise for a more just and sustainable economy. SVN promotes new models and leadership for socially and environmentally sustainable business in the twenty-first century. Job listings come from a diverse group of socially responsible companies and range from corporate CEOs to retail associates.

Energy.gov

Here you can learn about workforce development and education efforts, information about energy-related careers, and job listings in renewable energy and energy efficiency. The Office of EERE (Energy, Efficiency & Renewable Energy) partners with federal and state programs as well as clean energy companies to help build a talented and knowledgeable workforce.

EnvironmentalCareer.com

ECC has been helping people work for a better environment since 1980. ECC assists individuals and employers alike, in matching top candidates with today's top green employers.

The number of jobs in America's emerging clean energy economy grew nearly two and a half times faster than overall jobs between 1998 and 2007, according to a report released by the Pew Charitable Trusts. Pew developed a clear, data-driven definition of the clean energy economy and conducted the first-ever hard count across all 50 states of the actual jobs, companies, and venture capital investments that supply the growing market demand for environmentally friendly products and services.

With the creation of the new green industry you need to be ready to move forward fast and keep an open mind because the green job movement is hot, hot, hot and poised for explosive growth. Don't be left out in the cold!

CHAPTER NINE

Working for Gen Y? Why Not!

"Parents often talk about the younger generation as if they didn't have anything to do with it."

—*Haim Ginott*

The adults of Generation Y are expected to earn up to $3 trillion by 2017, even with a rocky economy creating havoc for two or three of those years. These 70 million adults born between 1979 and the mid-1990s want and need a variety of products and services from tattoos to technology. If you're young—or young at heart—you can make some serious cash from these new kids on the block. By planning and investing in a relationship with these young adults now, as they finish college and climb out of debt, this generation might very well take care of you in your old age.

But what does Gen Y want?

The adults of Generation Y, also called "millennials," are a potent and growing force in the economy. Even during a recession they are creating lucrative opportunities for almost everyone. But just because you were young once, doesn't mean you "get them."

It's important that you understand this group before they'll hand over any of their hard-earned cash (or granny's inheritance). Generation Y is the most tech-savvy and diverse group in American history. Odds are you've raised your own Gen Y kids and taught them that they can do everything and anything. These are the same kids we drove to soccer/dance/volleyball/karate and everything else under the sun. We told them they were *all* winners, so they're not about to be losers now, no matter how bad the economy. Most of all, these kids have game. They want and expect customized products and services to characterize their own unique styles. If you can figure out what they want—and give it to them—you'll have it made.

How do you reach these young consumers? How do you catch their attention with your idea/invention/career idea? Facebook. MySpace. Twitter. Digg. YouTube. IM. And Delicious. If you don't know what these are, you better learn fast before something new comes along. This generation lives in an age of information, but they don't get their ideas or news from books, TV, or the media. They get them from social networks. They get them from their friends. You want them to buy your products or hire you? Figure out how to catch their eye through these networks. The young adults have different aspirations and characteristics from their Gen X predecessors. You need to hang out and listen to them; just don't be creepy about it. For the most part, these consumers are street smart and savvy. They've already experienced some crazy things, including September 11. Don't try to fool them and, most of all, respect them. Then go for their wallet!

The Big Picture

Generation Y has a slew of fast, efficient resources to connect with one another. They spread the buzz, exchange information, and shop on a global level. With an Internet driven culture and worldwide social networking applications at their fingertips, there is no geographical limit for these consumers. It has never been easier to spend money on anything, anywhere. What's more, the youngest Gen Y consumers who have jobs such as babysitting or working at the water park don't have to dig into their parent's wallet for a credit card; they have other means to pay for goods and services such as Cybermoola.com, RocketCash.com, Doughnet.com, and iCanBuy.com, which are totally safe. These services are a "same as cash" option for shopping online. Companies such as RocketCash offer currency, which can be purchased by using a credit card or sending in a money order or check. Once a customer has purchased RocketCash, he goes through the RocketCash shopping portal to the merchant of his choice to select merchandise and make a purchase. RocketCash acts as a proxy server for the merchant, and when the customer is ready to check out, RocketCash automatically populates the checkout forms with customer data, like an e-wallet. (Not only are these companies a way to offer this young generation a way to buy your products, but they are companies you might consider working for.) The old standby, PayPal .com, even has a friendly name. These online e-commerce services that enable people all over the world to buy and sell to each other have more clout than cash. Remember these tips if you are considering setting up an online retail store for Generation Y.

On a global scale, the Gen Y market is larger and more accessible than ever. But its virtues also are its challenges. Emerging technology and competition for consumer dollars are swiftly changing. This generation is smart and loves instant gratification. Keeping ahead of the changes and capitalizing on them is a key priority if you want to work for them in one way or another. Understanding how millennials communicate, their social behaviors, and the technology and language they use is a critical factor for success.

Popurls.com: A Bird's-Eye View

It might be easy to feel overwhelmed by the fragmented maze of links, Web sites, chat rooms, and the ever multiplying possibilities serving millennials. An interesting place to start is by surveying a snapshot of the millennials' Internet world at large.

Visit popurls.com, which somehow stands for: popular URLs. Huh? Who knew, right? This site is a bird's-eye view of all the most popular media and social networking Web sites in the *world*. You can learn a lot about the habits, tastes, and needs of Generation Y by digging through the sites listed and, hence, figure out how to market and sell to these young folk.

Take your time weaving your way through the sites and sampling all the cool stuff on popurls. The creation of Austrian Web maverick Thomas Marban, popurls is one of the most comprehensive sites that ventures beyond the usual hangouts like MySpace. Each Web site on popurls has a job and career tab. Click the tabs for sites such as Digg and REDDIT, and find out who and what runs the world today.

Learning the needs of companies that service today's generation will lead you to ideas for a business you can start or a new job that excites you.

In many cases, there are links on company home pages where you can find out which venture capitalists funded the Web site and who created it. Take note of these venture capitalists in the event you may be inspired to develop an online business. Online, everyone is approachable. If you send someone an e-mail, chances are you'll get a prompt reply.

Digging through popurls and similar sites, you'll get a fast education and a reality check that will inspire ways to reinvent yourself while you learn new skills.

How to Identify Careers in the Gen Y Market

Start your career strategy in this sector by asking:

- Who are these people, and what do they want?
- What's missing in their lives that I can provide?
- How cool do I have to be?

Based on your answers, you can target the industries, products, and services described in this chapter as places to begin exploring your possibilities.

Talk Is Cheap—Not!

Before you decide to make a splash in this lucrative, exploding market, familiarize yourself with modern language. If a coworker or client says, "Are you dipping?" you might feel like a deer caught in the headlights. (Translation: this means they are asking you if you're leaving. But you knew that, right?)

Do you know the difference between an IM and a DM? Think of it like the difference between instant coffee and brewed coffee. You'll get instant-messaged for a live, online conversation in real time, but if there isn't time for live chat, a direct message (not live) will suffice. One thing for sure, get used to communicating in ways that don't involve talking to someone in person.

At the very least, know how Generation Y relates to you and to each other, so it's not weird for you to reply to their terms and adopt them for yourself.

UrbanDictionary.com is the best place to learn modern language. It's a fun, free up-to-the-minute Wikipedia-style dictionary that's written and kept up to date by the general public. *Time* magazine voted UrbanDictionary.com one of the 50 best Web sites of 2008. It's no coincidence that UrbanDictionary is one of the most popular sites visited by people who work in offices. Seriously. Check it out; you could be on the phone with a client who says, "Sorry it took me so long to text you that order. I had to use my Brickberry." You can simply reply, "No worries!" followed by "Hey, can I put you on hold for a second?" You won't be the first person to look up "Brickberry" in the Urban Dictionary while your client is on hold and find out that a Brickberry is an older model phone you have to use when your BlackBerry breaks. Composing a text message takes a long time on a Brickberry—sometimes more than a minute or two and time's a-wastin'! (If you own one, it's time to toss that dinosaur and order unlimited text messaging on your BlackBerry cell phone plan.)

Companies aimed at marketing to millennials and attracting Gen Y employees incorporate an informal, shorthand language in their communication. Sites like Digg and Twitter use some of this informal shorthand in their career and job listing section. For example, at Twitter.com company benefits are described as "bennies." If a coworker or human resource person says, "This company offers great bennies," don't be shocked. She is referring to health insurance and 401(k)s—not amphetamine pills containing the stimulant drug Benzedrine, which people called "bennies" back in the twentieth century.

Ontology—the study of human design—tells us that reality is created first with language. If this is true, and everything in the world arises from the language we use to define ideas and create new realities out of possibilities, then it might not be a bad idea to be dipping for work and loving the bennies.

To successfully profit from the Gen Y market, you don't have to memorize the UrbanDictionary or be afraid that you won't know what people are trying to say to you. But learning the psychographics of a market—how your market thinks, feels, reacts, and makes buying decisions—*is* a must.

Top Industries Aimed at Making a Profit from Generation Y

- Market research
- Employment and recruiting
- Food and alcoholic beverages
- Holistic and alternative medicines
- Entertainment, arts, and leisure
- Education—private and public
- Viral marketing
- Information industries

Top Careers for Generation Y to Explore for Opportunities

- Nongovernment agencies
- Biotech industries
- Hip information companies such as Yelp, Google, and Apple
- Teaching abroad
- Viral marketing and advertising
- Entertainment, arts, and leisure
- Social work
- Politics

Information Is a Hot Commodity

Were you ever envious of the California Gold Rush? Back in the 1800s people could simply *go* to California and gather gold because . . . it was *there*. Anyone who had a pan, a shovel, and the nerve to grab it could profit. Get ready for some exciting news: the gold rush is here again. But this time it's not in the dirt and you can't die of yellow fever looking for it. Information about millennials is gold. Companies desperately need to find out how their Web sites are fairing, what Generation Y wants, how these consumers react to products and services, and what compels their decisions. Careers in market research and Web site testing are burgeoning with millennials, and their lifestyles are driving the demand.

Why is market research more important today? Members of Gen Y are unlike any other generation in the way they choose their purchases. They do not respond positively to the status and image advertising tactics of the past. If a company isn't tapped into the minds of Generation Y, untold revenues could be lost and the company itself could fail miserably. Market research is about helping a business make profitable decisions. Behavioral and attitudinal data is used to help make the right decisions that will maximize profitability.

Information is gold. And it's *everywhere.* Anyone can gather and sell it, because it's *there.* And it's free. The demand for information about millennials is ongoing and huge. This demand is sourced by a diverse, rapidly changing, Internet-driven market.

Consider Sheri's story: Sheri, a 48-year-old, single mom of four millennials ranging from 13 to 24, was fired from her management position with a focus group department of a major pet food chain. Her entire department was eliminated. They were replaced with the outsourced services of an independent company that organizes and runs focus groups of consumers for product testing and market research. With two kids in college and two high school students heading to college, Sheri spent months skimping by on her unemployment checks and researching ways to start a business using her skills.

With the help of SCORE, a branch of the Small Business Administration that offers free business advice from retired executives, Sheri started her own market research company. She now gathers and sells information to companies that sell products for young people. The business was started with $50 for a domain name and Web site host.

Sheri's sons and daughters provided her most valuable resource. They organized their friends into "street teams" that surveyed fellow students to gather their opinions, desires, and reactions to certain products. No money needed to be spent on paper, expensive mailings, advertising, or telemarketing. "All of my surveys were conducted online via live chat, instant messaging, direct messaging, and text messaging," Sheri said.

"I began building my client base and started selling information to a range of companies and market research firms. My kids and their friends helped me reach out to millennials all over the world using viral marketing (the spreading of messages via video clips, text messages, e-books, and more), free online advertising publications, and social networking sites to get the word out. I was able to attract opinions from these Gen Yers, as well as their parents."

Sheri discovered that a growing number of companies, including Coca-Cola, Universal Studios, and McDonald's, used street teams comprised of young people to carry out their market research. The teams hang out in clubs, parks, and malls talking to teens about everything from fashion to finance, trying to target and capture trends as they materialize.

Given the fact that every year, four million new millennials are coming of age and shopping for their first cars, their first homes, and their first mutual funds, any and all information that helps companies decide how to advertise, design, and develop their products and services to Generation Y will be a hot commodity in the coming years.

Sheri now has a perpetually changing crew of 30 high school and college students working for her as interns and employees. The turn-over of people working for her has been great for garnishing new ideas and sources of information. Sheri grosses more than a million dollars per year providing consumer information to makers of everything from energy drinks to video games to sports wear to music and entertainment to fashion and cars. "Without my kids, it never would have dawned on me that there was such a huge need for market research in the young people's market," she said. "I still would be trying to figure out what people would buy for their cats and dogs. And most likely unemployed."

> *"Without my kids, it never would have dawned on me that there was such a huge need for market research in the young people's market."*

The importance of acquiring feedback and opinions is evident on every Web site, online news report, video, and blog that invites people to make comments on what they have just seen and experienced. Forums, message boards, polls, and discussions are available, and most Web sites include features that allow users to socially interact, express opinions, and share their experiences. The information fields are ripe for harvesting.

Conducting basic market research can be as simple as reading the comments and opinions posted online. They can be gathered, studied, organized, analyzed, and sold to marketing companies, or used to create a market research service. Did somebody say something you want to find out more about? No problem. E-mail them your questions. Begin a dialogue. Most people who post comments can be contacted via e-mail. Social networking really is the ability of the world to communicate. Using open source management systems that allow for fast and easy communication creates a vast arena for job opportunities and profitable freelancing and entrepreneurial ventures.

Tell a Friend!

Collecting information, getting the word out, and connecting with people is now a one-stop shop. Telling a friend no longer is a series of links that lead people away from the Web site they started on. That's thanks to "tell-a-friend" modules like SocialTwist.com, which is a box that contains several social networking links a person can use to forward videos, e-mails, and recommendations without being redirected away from the Web site they're visiting. You can get this tool free and use it to promote your services or business. Information can be shared, promoted, and branded with one button. Comments, opinions, and recommendations are today's gold. They reflect the demographic and psychographic information companies need.

Quirks.com is a comprehensive site about market research. Here you can find more than 7,000 market research companies to check out, listings of job openings, articles, definitions of market research terms, industry events, Webinars, and market research degree programs.

At Quirks, you can browse focus group facilities, research software titles, investigate market research panels and mystery shopping companies, and garner everything you need to familiarize yourself with this hot industry.

Technology and Applications: Tools for Living

Visit Gizmodo.com for an eye-popping look at the latest gadgets, accessories, phones, and gizmos that enable a person to have more fun communicating, sitting in front of a computer, or listening to music. Every product listed on Gizmodo features a comment section where viewers post their raves and/or scathing remarks.

Jobs related to tech products and communication devices can range from sales to marketing and advertising to product development and distribution. We may see companies fail that are peddling the same old stuff, but new technology and improved, more stylish versions of existing staples capture attention and buyers from all over the world.

Consider what happened to Mark. The 35-year-old furniture designer, was let go from a company in North Carolina that filed Chapter 11. "My back was killing me the day they let me go," Mark said. "All I could think of was, 'great, now I don't have to spend another day sitting in a chair in front of a computer.'" He spent his first day as an out-of-work furniture designer relaxing in his recliner at home. Mark eventually did go back to work, but he never left his chair. He designed an extremely comfortable, swanky-looking lounge chair with a built-in feature to accommodate a laptop. The chair allows a person to use a laptop while getting plenty of lumbar support. "You can recline and put up your feet," Mark said. "I don't know why the company I worked for never came up with the idea of making comfortable, cool-looking lounge chairs where you can spend all day working at a computer without getting a backache. No wonder they went bankrupt."

> *"All I could think of was, 'great, now I don't have to spend another day sitting in a chair in front of a computer.'"*

Employment and Recruiting

A survey in 2008 by Robert Half International says that nearly one out of every two business executives is concerned about the upcoming exodus of baby boomers from the workforce. The next big wave of workers, the millennial generation, will need to be recruited. However, as millennials become employees, a growing concern recurs. According to Bruce Tulgan, founder of Rainmaker Thinking, author of *It's Okay to Be the Boss*, and expert on young talent in the workplace: "Companies are having a hard time retaining and managing young employees." That is the number one finding. Tulgan, who has been interviewing managers and young people since 1993, concludes that the workplace is becoming more high pressure and the workforce is becoming more high maintenance.

These "kidployees," are hardworking and enthusiastic, but they won't settle for just any job. There are significant differences between Gen Yers and the older Gen Xers and baby boomers. The younger generation know that they can get hired by a variety of firms and have their pick of opportunities. So, rather than asking themselves if they're qualified, like older generations did, they instead turn the tables and ask employers why their place of employment is better than the one across the street. This generation is poised to do great things and lead wonderful lives. They're confident, comfortable with technology, and community oriented, and they want to make an impact immediately upon starting a new position.

To find out more about careers in recruiting, training, and managing young talent, visit Workforce.com, TheOrrellGroup.com, and Employee Evolution.com, an online community and career center for Generation Y. EmployeeEvolution consults and speaks with organizations on best practices for recruiting and retaining Generation Y and how to effectively use social media to reach a target market.

If you're 25 or under thinking, "Hey! What about me?" read on. The two best blogs—PenelopeTrunk.com and BrazenCareerist.com—are for and about you. Cofounder and author of *Employee Evolution* Ryan Healy blogs about Generation Y, management, personal development, entrepreneurship, and how organizations can effectively use social media. The aforementioned sites are well worth checking out for some eye-opening ideas about how Gen Y intends to change the working world and the workplace.

Education

The millennials are one of the most educated generations yet, and they love to learn. Going to college is no longer reserved for the elite, it is the norm. Today, 64 percent of women and 60 percent of men go to college after graduating high school, and 85 percent attend full time, according to the U.S. Bureau of the Census: Educational Attainment.

Learning from Our Children

This is a time when young people are working alongside people old enough to be grandparents. This creates both a clash of views and a necessary cooperation between generations. Generation Y workers do not want to be seen as children. Generation Yers think that they can show others a few things when it comes to work. Generational relations can be rough. Both sides of the generational spectrum are dismissive of the other's abilities. This is where the tension is created. There can be a market for helping employers (and families) learn how to manage these highly connected, supremely tech-savvy young people.

A mother and son team created a wildly successful consulting business to help companies retain their Generation Y employees and gain the most benefit from working with them. Terry was a 47-year-old former human resources executive living on her severance pay from a company that gave her the boot. Her 22-year-old son, Hunter, saved Terry's e-mails asking for insights on what was making the young people quit and why the older employees resented them. Hunter came up with an idea. "After hearing my mom's complaints it became clear that the two generations have totally different attitudes. They don't get each other," Hunter said. "After talking about it with my mom, I figured out a way to explain the differences. Then I invited her to start a consulting company with me."

"It was a brilliant idea," Terry said. She jumped on board with Hunter. Then they wrote grant proposals and received one that helped them launch an ad campaign geared toward companies that looked like they could follow success models like Google and Zappos—companies that have a strong retention rate and are reaping the advantages of being led by Gen Y innovators. "So much of upper management seems to underestimate the power of Generation Y's youth and optimism," Hunter said. "In my opinion management can be losing out on the massive potential of a generation that's confident and tech-savvy. My mom and I educate companies on how Generation Y can lead them into the future. They need to remember that people with years of experience didn't create Google or Facebook, young entrepreneurs did." Terry and Hunter are booked for the next 12 months educating clients on how to create a productive work environment where all three generations can happily co-exist.

If you're a therapist adapting to the Gen Y market, you may find yourself offering variable-length sessions instead of the standard 50 minutes, adding e-therapy (online sessions via Webcam), or pay-per-e-mail sessions to your mix of services. In the post–9/11 years with high rates of depression, post-war trauma, burned-out families, divorce, anxiety, and economic crisis, a career as a therapist for Gen Y will take on different formats. Thanks to technology, you might save a life or even a thousand lives.

It Pays to Be a Geek

If "viral" sounds like something you need to wash up after using, don't be alarmed; it isn't. It's a marketing strategy that relies on individual people rather than traditional campaigns to pass along a message to others. It's an idea that spreads. It usually refers to marketing on the Internet. Viral marketing takes its name from its messages that use "hosts" to spread themselves rapidly, like a biological virus. Hotmail, for example, or YouTube are both big components of viral marketing. The more people use them, the more people see them. The more people see them, the more people use them. The product or service must be something that improves once more people use it. Simple, right? Don't believe us? Check this out: viral marketing, also known as buzz marketing or avalanche marketing, turned the *Twilight* books—young adult vampire books—into mega-hits. The author and publisher used tools such as BlogTalkRadio, Twitter, Facebook, and MySpace to push the books toward the core audience: teenagers. And it worked. Sequel books, movies, T-shirts, video games—everything and anything that has to do with young vampires—is a hit with people of all ages! Go figure. Go viral.

Word of mouth and viral marketing are popular and effective. If you've ever received a video someone sent you from YouTube, or posted or responded to someone's comments in a forum, the "virus" has spread to you. If you like what the other person sends, you will most likely forward it to your friends. This is viral marketing, and it's spreading like the plague . . . in a good way!

Many moments of success await the viral marketing ninja who can capture the intrigue of millennials. Surveys show that Gen Y responds positively because it's honest and gives consumers the perspective from an unbiased individual.

Now that the Internet is available to more than six billion people worldwide and counting, viral marketing has had astonishing effects for pushing products, goods, services, and raising awareness. Recent studies show that 74 percent of the U.S. population uses the Internet as a primary source to get information. This percentage is the highest among other traditional sources of information, including professional advisors, newspapers, and magazines. Therefore, marketers have a great advantage when it comes to exploiting the Internet, because of its long reach. As far as viral marketing goes, the Internet is a gold mine for targeting specific niche audiences; even the fickle Gen Yers, especially now with all the social networking sites available. With use of the Internet, viral marketing can take on many faces to spread the word.

Gen Y consumers not only want to acquire a product or service information from a company's Web site, they want to be able to discuss it among themselves and glean information from others who have experienced that product or service.

A growing number of companies are retaining the services of bloggers and viral marketers. By starting forums, blogs, and social networking, companies realize they can achieve a state of popularity with "reality based" advertising. For example, Audi once staged a car theft scene from a dealership in New York and sent the video out on YouTube. People were very intrigued by these events and started talking about it, blogging about it, and posting videos and other user-generated media. Audi managed to attract campaign-zealous followers who would show up at the dealership and post flyers to help recover the stolen car. They waited eagerly for updates on the thickening plot.

Viral marketers say Gen Y is tired of irrelevant ads bombarding them from every direction. With the availability of viral media, companies are seeking people who can dream up creative ways to position themselves in this new culture of online communities and retain interest while building communities.

If you're attracted to the marketing field, check out ClickZ.com, Suite101.com, and GoEcart.com to get some ideas on how to keep a viral marketing campaign relevant and interesting.

Entertainment, Arts, and Leisure

The Gen Yers are mainly responsible for killing off newspapers and television. Some of them are the most coveted TV advertising markets—the 14- to 25-year-old age group of the millennials watches an average of 10.5 hours of TV a week—unlike the older generation who watches five hours more each week. So who's the couch potato now, Mom and Dad?

But it's not like this generation is outside playing hacky-sack. Nope. They're still glued to a screen of sorts, be it movie or computer.

Five years after YouTube exploded onto the scene, the video-hosting site is still searching for a reliable monetization method. The future of online video content will be free TV, such as what Hulu.com delivers now. What's more, this generation won't sit at their desk to have TV Web access; they'll watch the shows on a mobile device. Yahoo!'s TV Widgets initiative (ConnectedTV.yahoo.com) aims to offer Internet-based content via TV. By partnering with entertainment companies,

Yahoo! plans to facilitate Web browsing while watching a favorite TV show or big sports game.

Tech-Centric Showbiz Careers

While jobs in this area still are being conceived, now is the time to jump over to Yahoo!—Careers.yahoo.com/ —for a job that may or may not have been created yet. But don't forget about jobs at Hulu—Hulu.com/jobs— the up-and-coming free TV site that includes everything from software developers to fancy-pants lawyers. (Look for information about these companies in the resource section of this book.)

And lest we forget, YouTube is a great place to express your creativity as well as earn cash to pay that mortgage; YouTube.com is where to begin your job search if you want to work for this fun company in the United States, Europe, or Asia. Hey, they even give you a free T-shirt and snacks with that big, fat paycheck.

Now more than ever, you need to set your job sights toward creating your own niche in this young world or look to create products aimed at Gen Yers. Are you a freelance writer? *Surfer* magazine out of San Clemente, California, has been around forever, and there's no stopping this wave of success! Check out Surfermagazine.com and Surfer Publications at SurfMag.com. These magazines are always on the lookout for great writers. Also, if you can somehow think like a teenage girl, why not write or sell advertising for "Tween" magazines, including Twist and M? BauerPublishing.com is the place to send your clips and resume.

As for movies, this generation still loves movies whether they watch on the big screen or at home via Netflix or Blockbuster. Many of these youngsters are into independent films as well as older movies, proven by an upswing of sales at small mom-and-pop independent movie rental stores. For jobs as customer service reps, human resource wonks, or IT specialists with Netflix, check out Netflix.com/job. If you're more old school and prefer Blockbuster, they have jobs, too.

If you haven't figured it out by now; the consumers with attitude are the "deciders." They are the most important age group for entrepreneurs.

This is the demographic that will create the jobs of the future. These dream consumers have $1 trillion in buying power, according to the U.S. Census Bureau, and they spend about $300 to $500 a month on entertainment alone. If you can come up with a game, Webcast, or product that would capture the attention span of this age group, not only will you be a survivor in this economy, you will also be a leader. Take the offensive, not the defensive, when searching for opportunities. This really is the market to capture. Even if you don't have an idea or a product to sell, find a job with a company that understands and even caters to this generation. You want to work for a video game company? Great. Besides the big organizations such as Sony and Nintendo, there are plenty of other companies that want your talents. Check out places such as BigFishGames.com, TrionWorld.com, or the great gaming job site SimplyHired.com.

Tips for Traveling Kids

Generation Y has insatiable wanderlust. They leave their jobs to back-pack through the mountains and glaciers of Patagonia and call in sick for a long weekend in Las Vegas because they probably still have fond memories of mom and dad schlepping them on family vacations through the Grand Canyon. Whatever the reason, this is one of the fastest-growing demographic segments in the travel industry today. A new research report released by Xola Consulting, Inc. indicates this group demands authentic travel experiences rich in cultural exchange and environmental immersion much like the baby boomers demand. They like to hike as well as spa *while* golfing and surfing. This group is well educated and has a more broad view of the world than other generations. They seek destinations and adventure travel opportunities outside the norm.

So what does that mean for the poor, sad, unemployed reader? It means jobs in the travel industry! Hello!

While travel agents are making a quiet comeback, travel Web sites can hardly keep up with demand. That, of course, means more jobs for you! Orbitz Worldwide has offices in Chicago, London, and pretty much all over the world. These folks offer jobs for laid-back accountants in not-so-laid-back Sydney, Australia, and sales management jobs in Paris, France. You gotta like that!

Do you want to forget about Wall Street and float down a river all day? Then check out CoolWorks.com, where you can find outdoor careers such as a kayak instructor, river guide, or traveling musician. Really—they actually have these types of jobs!

Do you have one of those bumper stickers on your soon-to-be-repossessed BMW that says: "A Lousy Day of Fishing Still Beats a Good Day at Work"? Here's your chance to walk the talk. Figure out how to start your own fishing guide business or find a river to work on. Go to TalaskaRiverAdventures.com to find jobs on the water.

With all the fishing and backpacking and globetrotting these youngsters seem to be able to afford, luggage companies are still doing well. Eagle Creek is a company with a conscience, and they just happen to make soft luggage, popular with Generation Y. Go to their site at EagleCreek.com to apply for a position. R.E.I. is an outdoor adventure store that caters to all ages, and Gen Y buys their travel gear mostly from this store and their Web site. For job inquiries visit REI.com.

This generation will travel whether the stock market has bottomed out or not, they have a job or not, or their mom gives them permission to leave the country or not. They're going to travel, and you can't stop them! If travel is your interest, you should be able to find a job (more of these great gigs in the resource section) in this industry. It's fun—you can usually go to work in shorts and you get a tan, all while making a few bucks.

Food for Thoughts

Although this is the generation who knows how much an iPhone retails for but not how much a loaf of bread costs, they can certainly spend their cash on food. These are the children we used to spoon-feed organic baby food that we stayed up all night sterilizing and canning in our kitchens. The same little ones we tried to forbid to consume sugar and soda. We can't blame them if their tastes are a little picky and elitist.

According to *USA Today*: "Their childhood, filled with planned activities, has extended into their adult lives, and they are very busy and over taxed. Twenty-eight percent describe their diets as unhealthy versus only 19 percent of the total shopper population; almost half of them wish they had time to exercise more versus a third of the total shopper population; and 29 percent say they smoke as compared to 19 percent of the total shopper population."

They want nutritious food and they want high-energy foods that make them feel good, but they don't want to give up the In-and-Out Burgers or their snacks. In fact, the Wharf Research Division of the Center for Culinary Development reports that this generation still likes to play with their food. Rip apart the Oreos. Crunch the soybeans. The research also points out that 27 percent of this demographic consumes either a snack or a meal between 10 p.m. and 5 a.m. Sixty-three percent, meanwhile, eat either a snack or a meal between 2 p.m. and 5 p.m. You don't need a PhD to figure out that this group's snacking offers a plethora of career and job opportunities.

A Healthy Diet of Money

If you want your next job to be more Zen-like than your previous gig, check out jobs at retail health food opportunities, for example:

- Whole Foods— WholeFoodsMarket.com
- Sprouts— Sprouts.com
- Trader Joes—TraderJoes.com

There are also plenty of sales gigs in the food industry, including:

- UNFI—UNFI.com
- Tree of Life—TreeOfLife.com
- Organic Valley Co-Op—OrganicValleyCoop.com

But it's not all about healthy foods for this group. Nope, they like their high-energy drinks and their adult beverages, just like mom and dad.

Companies such as Red Bull (RedBull.com) need help, from accounting to quality assurance. So get some wings and check them out! Monster Energy is owned by Coca-Cola (TheCoca-ColaCompany.com). Thinking about how many career opportunities they have going for them makes us dizzy.

While the vitamin water and energy drink is still hyperactive in the market, anti-energy drinks are now popping up, possibly to counteract all the wired teens and young adults out there. There's the "anti-energy" drinks such as Drank (DrankBeverage.com), which guarantees to "slow your roll." This is a new market, and jobs are being created as we write.

When it's all said and done though, beer remains the beverage of choice for millennials. On a dollar basis, beer accounts for 47 percent of Gen Y alcoholic beverage spending, and on a volume basis, 83 percent of purchases. Millennials are almost twice as likely as older consumers to purchase imported beers, and almost three times as likely to pick up a craft beer.

Stone Brewery (StoneBrew.com) touts itself as the "All-time top brewery on earth!" New Belgium Brewery (NewBelgium.com), out of Colorado, advertises job posts such as "Carnival Technician," a sort-of traveling beer roadie, as well as "Idaho Beer Ranger," which turns out to be a sales position in Idaho. Who knew?

Looking for retail sales? Then Beverages & More on the West Coast is the place to apply (BevMo.com). Or just come up with your own beer brand by crafting the ale in your own basement. Check out Brewpoll (Brewpoll.com) to learn how, and bottoms up!

We don't know how to say it any more clearly: don't wait for times to get better, take this time to become a survivor—and a successful survivor at that. By keeping up with the latest Gen Y trends, you have a leg up on all the other mainstream job seekers.

CHAPTER TEN

Banking on Boomers

"Age is an issue of mind over matter. If you don't mind, it doesn't matter."

—Mark Twain

Ahh, the baby boomer generation. This is a group that may be even more spoiled than Generation Y. After all, when World War II ended and the GIs came home, they quickly got to work—having kids. Mom and dad were happy as hell that the world hadn't ended, and so these children were handed the world on a silver platter. What's more, the boomers expected the good luck to continue until the generation died out like the *Tyrannosaurus rex.*

Change of plans!

Here's how it went all haywire: in the 1960s and '70s, the boomers held sit-ins, love-ins, food-ins, and whatever else they could do sitting down while becoming the center of attention. Back then the world couldn't do a thing about their teenage revolution and Flower Power. These long-haired hippies were suddenly in charge, and mom and dad could only see doom and gloom in their offsprings' future. Then, in the 1980s the boomers surprised everyone and cut their hair and shaved their legs. And they wanted more, more, and even more! Gone were the granny dresses and love beads. Now it was all about foreign cars and power suits, implants, and buying the biggest and gaudiest tract homes they could find, which helped drive real estate prices sky high.

So, for the past 60 years it's been all about them. Their powerful effect on Wall Street can't be denied, even in these tough times, but their effect on consumerism has driven many companies' earnings up and will continue to do so until the last boomer has gone to rock 'n' roll heaven.

Boomers were born between 1946 and 1964, and many were born to parents who grew up during the Great Depression. For the most part, baby boomers have never truly experienced any financial woes—until now.

There is good news: with the baby boomer generation making up more than one-third of the U.S. population, they represent a total income estimated to be well over $900 billion—give or take a billion or two after the recession hit. Boomers still are the wealthiest, best educated, and most sophisticated purchasers, not to mention well preserved, and they represent a dramatic 40 percent of total consumer demand. Realistically, these ex-hippies still have money to spend, and even if they don't have the money, there are products they need, so they find the cash.

Today the baby boomer generation controls nearly 70 percent of the total net worth of American households and owns 80 percent of all the money in savings and loan associations—even in this economy. These boomers just "keep on truckin'"!

Consider the case of Bob. He sold advertising for several different radio stations in Cincinnati and later in South Florida. In South Florida the station he worked for was eventually sold. Six months after the merger a new sales manager, who was 27 years old with only five years of sales experience, was hired. Bob was 56, with almost 20 years' experience selling radio advertising. The new sales manager decided Bob wasn't a "team player," so he fired him. "Within a month I was working at another radio station," Bob said. "After about nine months into my job, my former sales manager was fired and got himself hired as the sales manager at the station where I found a job. Since he figured I wasn't a 'team player' previously, he fired me again!"

After the second firing Bob decided he had had enough. He started his own advertising agency with personal funds and the help of a few loyal customers from his days of selling radio. "My business took off, and my agency is still in operation," he said. "I have experience, and that comes with age. Either way you look at it, I didn't give up."

But just so you know we're not looking at this age group through rose-colored glasses, here's a dose of reality. In December 2008, a Harris Interactive and Principal Financial Group online survey of 1,179 employees and 625 age 60-plus found that two-thirds of workers and 59 percent of current retirees have reduced their spending over the previous two months because of fear over the economy, job stability, or rising prices. But then again, who hasn't? The top areas for cutbacks were media subscriptions, gym memberships, land-line phone services, lawn services, and television services, so if you're not a huge cable corporation or a gardener (but really, how long can these folks continue to push a lawn mower?), you're golden.

Since the economy began to flounder, more boomers have started figuring out how to have a "do-over." They are looking to pursue the dreams they put on hold to raise families and make the big bucks. Now they're trying to turn their passion into "encore" careers. Encore careers are defined as those that combine income, meaning, and social purpose. They include jobs in the medical, education, and nonprofit sectors, including teaching, social entrepreneurs, and nursing. "These are fields already facing job shortages," says Marc Freedman, CEO of Civic Ventures, in his book, *Encore: Finding Work That Matters in the Second Half of Life*. Dentists are retiring to become photographers, doctors are becoming consultants, firefighters are becoming forest rangers, and professors are teaching kindergarten because the one thing boomers can do is accept a challenge.

WorkForce50.com is a career site that serves older workers by listing jobs placed by employers specifically interested in staffing from the over-50 workforce. The site also features education resources that cater to mature workers in transition who are searching for employment. Monster.com features a special section dedicated to careers at 50 plus, and KitHayes.com offers updates and advice on how people can transform from retired to rewired.

Older workers are delaying retirement in growing numbers. They want to continue to earn money and fulfill their dreams. If you're thinking of launching a blog or Web site that helps boomers find their next career, you might attract a huge crowd.

Retirement Is a Dirty Word

The jobs are out there for folks 55 and older and not just as school crossing guards or greeters at Wally World. Check out this report put out in 2008 by the Urban Institute:

20 Hot Jobs for Older Workers

Occupation	2007 Employment	Projected 10-Year Growth, %	Share of Workers 55 and Older, %
Personal and home-care aides	794,846	50.7	23.4%
Personal financial advisers	343,170	40.9	18.8
Veterinarians	66,824	35.5	22.4
Social and community service managers	340,736	24.6	24.4
Miscellaneous entertainment attendants	163,717	23.8	21.1
Surveyors, cartographers, and photogrammetrists	42,128	23.6	16.9
Environmental scientists and geoscientists	102,766	23.6	20.2
Registered nurses	2,608,762	23.4	17.9
Animal trainers	45,072	23.3	23.0
Instructional coordinators	24,165	23.3	32.0
Locksmiths and safe repairers	25,047	23.1	25.4
Postsecondary teachers	1,357,642	22.8	27.0
Archivists, curators, and museum technicians	56,396	22.2	24.7
Social workers	728,481	22.2	17.5
Management analysts	662,978	22.0	26.5
Pharmacists	229,830	21.8	21.4
Counselors	707,527	21.4	18.2
Business operation specialists	100,367	20.9	18.8
Brokerage clerks	3,831	20.5	29.5
Religious workers	109,127	20.5	32.5

Source: Urban Institute

Many of these jobs require going back to school, but what the hell, you're not doing anything anyway. You may as well buy some school supplies and get yourself to college. Here are a few schools that offer accelerated courses as well as online classes; start your school search at: Phoenix.edu.com, NU.edu.com (National University), and eLearners .com.

Bing, Bang, Boom-er!

Here are some of the more creative jobs boomers are dreaming about, according to RetirementJobs.com:

- Art dealer
- Male Avon lady
- BMW test driver
- Christmas tree farmer
- Comedian
- Executive assistant
- Feng shui consultant
- Funeral director
- Genetic counselor
- Hair stylist
- Historical re-enactor
- Homestead farmer
- Major league usher
- Massage therapist
- Movie critic
- Preschool teacher
- Snowplow driver
- Travel writer
- Venture coach
- Yoga instructor
- ZAMBONI driver

A Boomer and His Money Soon Are Parted

Plenty of baby boomers still have a tidy nest egg, and there are plenty of ways to make money from this age group without knocking them over and stealing their purses. You can be any age to dip into their wallets as long as you have an idea and tenacity.

Ralph was 60 when he decided he needed to come up with extra income. For most of his life he had worked for a health food company, running their stores, hiring and firing employees, and buying and merchandising health food—pretty much toeing the company line. His wife (full discloser—his wife is coauthor Candice Reed, not to toot her own horn) was a writer, and together they raised two children in a funky, ranch-style home in Southern California. Both were looking forward to a retirement of travel. Of course, so were the millions of other baby boomers. When the financial meltdown began, Ralph and his wife took a hit. Ralph was replaced in his job by the owner's son, so he took a job that paid a quarter of what he had been making, mainly for the health benefits. His wife was working for three large newspapers as a freelancer and making plenty of money, and the kids were gone so they felt comfortable; they didn't need a huge paycheck. Fast-forward to 2008.

"Newspapers died almost overnight," Ralph said. "My wife went from making a decent salary to almost nothing in just a few months. The outlook was pretty gloomy."

While Ralph's wife picked up a few writing gigs here and there, he tried to think of what they could do to get back to their retirement dream of traveling and meeting people.

"One day we were drinking cocktails with friends and discussing our predicament," Ralph explained. "After a couple more drinks, someone suggested we turn our house into a bed and breakfast [B&B]. We laughed about it then, but the next day my wife looked at me and said, 'Let's do it.' The more we thought about our own great experiences staying in B&Bs here and in Europe, combined with my wife's love of cooking and entertaining, the more we thought the idea might work."

The couple bought a book on starting a B&B, researched endlessly on the Internet, and talked to some B&B owners. Then they went on a cleaning spree. With not much money in the bank, they resorted to painting and even bringing in three tons of rocks from the beach to landscape their yard. Then they threw out anything and everything they didn't need, condensing four rooms into three. "We figured that if we had to sell the house, at least we were ahead of the game," Ralph said laughing. "Besides, we knew we would eventually get old and have to move into "the home." Our kids would appreciate it if we threw some of the crap away before they had to do it."

Ralph and his wife designed a Web site, installed PayPal, and began to spread the word. They joined Bed&Breakfast.com for a fee, checked out their local zoning rules, bought a business license, and waited for the phone to ring. Ring it did.

"Boomers like me were still looking to travel in this terrible economy, but they didn't want to spend a fortune," he said. "Also a lot of people my age love B&Bs, and they enjoy meeting people and learning about how others live and travel. Right from the beginning it was a good fit." The couple worked hard, doing all the cleaning and cooking. In four months' time, business was so good they had to turn away people.

"Are we going to get rich from this business? No. But we were never about that," Ralph said. "We can, however, make the house payment and actually close up for a few days a month to travel. It's working out great. It's hard work and isn't for everyone, but it's the perfect retirement job for us. The idea was hatched during a night of drinking, but when we sobered up we realized it was the perfect plan."

While many people dream of opening a bed and breakfast, it's not just pancakes and O.J. To find out how to open your own B&B, check out these sites:

> BusinessplanWorld.com offers links to sites regarding business.
>
> OpenABedAndBreakfast.com and InnkeepingShow.com offer courses and guidance so you don't send the guests running for the local Motel 6.

Let the Good Times Keep on Rollin'

Baby boomers for the most part are an optimistic bunch. They've always had that peace and love and woo-woo kind of spirit that their parents didn't have and the younger kids seem to be missing. Baby boomers are all about the future, but as far as products go, many of them still want to hold onto their glory days. They enjoy the kind of music they listened to when they were practicing their "free love" or going to dances in their bell-bottoms. According to most consumer profiles, baby boomers make up nearly one-third of the total music-buying market, but they're not so much into down-loading. They still buy it and listen to it on their stereos. If you have knacks for compiling tunes and want to create your own online music store, check out CDbaby.com and SilverlakeMusic.com. Peruse these sites and take the best information to design your own music CDs to sell.

Baby boomers definitely use the Internet and they like to shop online, but they're much different than Generation Y when it comes to buying on the Internet. They own all the latest high-tech gadgets, but for the most part, they can't even hook up the cable box without help from their kids. Geek Squad has plenty of job opportunities for tech-savvy . . . umm, geeks. Their site is GeekSquad.com, but there are others such as Fast-teks (Fasttcks.com). Better yet, if you have the tools, the high-water pants, and the ability to fix computers, start your own in-home computer repair service; learn how to spread the word in Chapter 14.

For the most part, this group has learned to save a dollar or two and can still afford the little luxuries in life. The trick is to figure out how you can get a piece of the baby boomer pie.

Consider the case of Penny, a baby boomer, who grew up in a home with almost no discretionary income. Her mother was divorced and her father paid $75 a month to support three children.

"We definitely knew the value of money," said Penny. "If something broke, we fixed it ourselves. If the house needed painting, we painted it. We made do. My mom was creative and liked a nice home. She often shopped at the Goodwill for a piece of furniture and brought it home, gave it a good paint job, and made something beautiful out of it. I remember the pride she had in these creations of hers."

Over the years, Penny and her husband created a successful company. For most of their marriage the money had been invested in growing the business, and so this computer-savvy boomer's favorite place to shop became eBay.

"I shop eBay for lots of reasons," she said. "In most instances you pay no tax. You can find almost anything you can imagine and at much lower prices than at the stores. Gas has been very expensive, so you don't waste gas. Delivery is way cheaper than the cost of the gas and the taxes you are saving. I've been very busy, and I save time by not having to go to shop."

Penny attends plenty of parties and fundraisers and she has to dress the part. She loves the clothes at Chico's, Ralph Lauren, Brighton, Dooney Burke, and Gucci. She is not, however, a fan of the prices.

"I've always enjoyed shopping designer resale for clothing, and you can monitor these items on eBay for great deals—some new, some resale. I have a closet full of clothes, purses, shoes, and jewelry bought on eBay for a fraction of the cost of retail," she said. Penny concludes that it doesn't make sense to waste money, even if you can afford to.

If you'd like to make some bucks off these types of boomers, set up your own cyber shop. There are literally millions of people online looking for items to buy, and it couldn't be easier to connect with them. Use existing venues or set up your own Internet store. (Learn how in this book.) You also can go to sites like Amazon.com, Webidz.com, or Half .com to sell used books and CDs; of course, there's always eBay. If you really don't want to sell it yourself, but you still want the moola, have the folks at Biddaboo.com do it for you—but be willing to pay.

The Summer of Love Never Ends

Baby boomers love life. Just because they've lost some of their stocks and have seen their 401(k)s dwindle doesn't mean they won't find the money for the things they want. It was that way from the beginning, and it will continue to be that way.

From the time his first song hit the charts, musician Jimmy Buffett became an icon of many baby boomers by offering them the ultimate tropical party vibe. But the leader of Margaritaville didn't kick back on an island getting stoned all the time, he cashed in on the party phenomenon.

Buffett has an estimated annual income of more than $40 million by shilling his merrymaking theme at his restaurants, his clothing line, his booze, and his casinos. Among the products he's involved with are Land-shark Lager, the Margaritaville, and Cheeseburger in Paradise restaurant chains, clothing and footwear, household items and drink blenders.

So what are his fans—who are mostly 50 and older—buying?

"I like the whole concept of not growing old and retiring to an island," said parrot-head Tom. "Who wouldn't want to wear shorts, sit on the beach, and drink margaritas all day?"

Buffett has figured out how to sell products beside music to these aging Peter Pans. Margaritaville boat shoes and flip-flops are found in shopping malls. Margaritaville Foods sells salsa, hummus, tortillas, and dips in Wal-Mart and other stores. Margaritaville tequila is in liquor stores all across the country. Jobs courtesy of Jimmy Buffett can be found at Maletis .com (Maletis Beverage) as well as Margaritaville.com.

> *"Who wouldn't want to wear shorts, sit on the beach, and drink margaritas all day?"*

"Jimmy Buffett and his team at Margaritaville have created an extraordinary brand instantly recognizable to an enormously large and dedicated fan base," said Richard Fields, CEO of Coastal Development, in an article to the Associated Press in 2009. "The brand implies quality, value, and good times."

Speaking of good times, boomers aren't the guys yelling, "You kids get off my lawn!" That would be their parents. This group still wants to have fun, and there are jobs for you aimed at their nonstop fun—from jumping out of airplanes (Skydive.com) to in-home sex toy parties (Secret-Treasures.com).

Boomers are the ones that made John, Paul, and Ringo rich. When the Fab Four ran off to join an ashram and practice yoga, so did many of the kids. As they grew up they didn't always have the time to practice the downward dog, but now that things have slowed a bit they are walking around with rolled-up mats on their backs muttering "*ommm.*" So where do you come in? A job of course! Yoga is hot. Yoga is cool. It's actually both, and you can earn bucks by teaching or buying up a studio or designing stretchy yoga pants that really, really stretch and, well, you get the drift. Check out these very calming Web sites for jobs in the yoga industry. Namasté!

To purchase a yoga studio, peruse YogaFinder.com; to buy into a yoga franchise, look at SunstoneYoga.com; and to find a relaxing job, look toward Giam.com.

Marketing to Boomers

Increasingly hip baby boomers like Penny could be the target for tech marketers during the next few years, according to a joint study by TNS Compete and the Consumer Electronics Association.

These consumers have become more comfortable with searching online, buying from Web sites, and purchasing high-definition televisions, fancy smart phones, and near-pocket-size PC computers, states the study, entitled "Greying Gadgets: How Older Americans Shop for and Use Consumer Electronics."

Boomer consumers ages 50 and older are as likely to own, or plan to purchase, a high-definition television as those ages 49 and younger. And 80 percent of 60-somethings used a cell phone in the past week—a rate similar to those ages 18 to 34. About 71 percent of 60-somethings and 52 percent of 70-somethings used a search engine in the past week, compared with 77 percent of those ages 18 to 34. But all the studies in the world won't make a boomer buy your concept or idea if you don't know how to speak to them. They want respect, and for the most part they don't want to be referred as "Dude" or "Man." They also want you to focus on them when you are waiting on them or trying to sell them something, so pay attention to what they want, and you'll make that sale.

The quest for self-discovery and self-actualization are fundamental midlife issues, and boomers resonate with marketing messages that help them process their lives. Boomers are increasingly seeking paths toward self-expression, while advancing agendas focused on balance, core values, and psychological self-reliance. A career as a life or media coach could be directed at this group. Holistic medicine and vitamins also are big boomer-sellers. Did you sell stocks and bonds in your former life? Well, as exciting as that may have been, perhaps a change to selling wheat grass juice and bee pollen might be more calming for you while putting a few shekels in your wallet. Did you work for an A-hole in your last job? Okay, take what you learned and become a colonic therapist! ColonHealth.net and NaturalHealers.com will teach you all you *never* wanted to know about colons.

Self-expression.com has information on becoming a life coach, and MarketingToBoomers.com is pretty much self-explanatory.

Selling to the Boomer Consumer

What is the best way to market to boomers and the mature market? Boomers and seniors are at completely different stages of their lives. It's important to identify which stages most closely align with your product or service.

- Do they have kids at home? Young or returned to the nest?
- Do they have parents at home?
- Are they healthy? What ailments do they have?
- Are they retired?
- Are they active?

Marketing to a boomer who is 60 is much different than marketing to boomer who is 50. Make sure you know what age group you want to work for before you head out the door.

Ten Marketer Commandments

When it comes to boomers today, Matt Thornhill, coauthor of *Boomer Consumer*, says there are 10 rules marketers must adhere to if they want to strike gold. "We haven't found ourselves needing to change or modify any of these rules," he says in his book. "They're not time-sensitive."

1. Treat everyone differently.
2. Use emotionally meaningful concepts, words, and images.
3. Be positive.
4. Realize that more information is better.
5. Tell a story.
6. Understand my changing values.
7. Make it relevant to me.
8. Play in the gray.
9. Use life stage, not age.
10. Learn, baby, learn.

Of course, if you're an actual baby boomer, you're already a step ahead of everyone else. You know how to market to *you*, right?

Traveling Isn't for Sissys

Boomers want to live out the last of their days as free spirited as they began. They want to create memories rich with ambiance and personal engagement. They are experience seekers—they always were, and they always will be until they are too hobbled to jump out of a plane or too blind to backpack through the Everglades. That's why the adventure travel and entertainment trends are gaining momentum, even in a sagging economy.

This Is How Boomers Roll

A company called Travel Marketing Decisions identifies 12 truths about baby boomers and their marketing implications for the industry. The boomers . . .

1. Consider travel a necessity, not a luxury
2. Have traveled more than their predecessors
3. See themselves as forever young
4. Want to have fun
5. Demand immediate gratification
6. Are not passive
7. Think they are special
8. Like creature comforts
9. Are time deprived
10. Will pay for luxury, expertise, and convenience
11. Are skeptical of institutions and individuals
12. Like to associate with people like themselves

The bottom line is, boomers will travel until they go on to their final resting place.

In a recent TripAdvisor survey, 73 percent of this age group said they plan to visit a national park in 2009, up from 62 percent one year ago. Thus, national parks will be a top trend for boomers looking for

vacations that will allow them to make some lifetime memori
a few pennies.

For exciting career opportunities outdoors, check out
NPS.gov (National Park Service Web site; keyword search:
CoolWorks.com, and Backdoorjobs.com.

Three-quarters of those polled in a Travel Industry Association
survey plan to book a package vacation to save cash, a trend that is particularly popular with baby boomers, according to the U.S. Tour Operators
Association. If you like to talk and you want to travel, check out job sites
for the tour guide industry: Zibb.com and Jobline.net/Traveljob.com.

More than one-third of U.S. respondents in the same TripAdvisor
survey say they will visit an environmentally friendly hotel or resort in
2009. Likewise, 32 percent of respondents say they will be more environmentally conscious in their travel decisions than they were the year
before. For a list of jobs at eco-friendly hotels check out Ecotrotters.com,
GreenHotels.com, and DoubletreeGreen.com.

The cruise industry is offering some of its lowest rates in history, and
boomers are climbing on board. If you want to fulfill your inner "Gopher
Smith," find out more about cruising jobs at Carnival.com, ShipJobs
.com, and CruiseLineJob.com, and set a course in the right direction.

Next, turn up the heat and tempt the taste buds because culinary
travel is sizzling hot for 2009. It's the top pick for 2009 Specialty Travel
Trends and Destinations by the Specialty Travel Agents Association
(STAA). Boomers are leading the way to the chow-line, so don't miss
out on an opportunity. The STAA says there is a growing demand for
travel that includes local cuisine and wine itineraries. Options worldwide
may include learning about food production, local market excursions,
cooking classes, wine tastings, and farm stays. It just so happens that you
can post your resume on any of these sites: WineBusiness.com, Tasting-
Wine.com, and FrenchCulinary.com.

General Hospital

The bad news for baby boomers is that they are getting old. Old means
failing parts and spare parts. The good news for you, if you are willing
to pick up the pieces, is that this aging process is creating jobs for just
about everyone.

Boomers are creating a demand for drugs, health services, and medical supplies. Healthcare today makes up 16 percent of the gross national product, which is three times the percentage of 1960, according to Kaiser Foundation. Job openings in the healthcare field continue to grow, according to a report from the Bureau of Labor Statistics. Since June 2007, healthcare has added 348,000 jobs. In June alone, 15,000 jobs were added in the field, with 13,000 in ambulatory services. But the numbers keep growing! According to the American Association for Retired Persons (AARP), there are currently 16,000 nursing homes in the United States, 39,500 assisted living facilities, 1,900 continuing care retirement communities, and 300,000 units of Section 202 Affordable Housing. The waiting list for Section 202s averages 13.4 months. Currently, there are 1.4 million nursing home residents, 900,000 residents in assisted living facilities (ALFs), 750,000 independent living residents, about 150,000 who use adult day services, and 1.4 million who utilize home health. But that's just today—only about half of the senior population anticipated for those facilities and services when the boomers hit 70 and 80!

Consider Aileen's story. She was a financial planner for 20 years and, although she loved the work, the hours and stress were burning her out. She wanted to give back, but she still needed a paycheck. She spent months searching for just the right direction to move toward and finally decided to become a healthcare franchisee.

> *"Since the first moment I started this business it's been a success, and it's restored my faith in humanity."*

"I thought of my parents who live on the other side of the country and wondered who would take care of them when the time came," said Aileen who lives in Southern California. "And it made perfect sense to switch careers. Since the first moment I started this business it's been a success, and it's restored my faith in humanity."

She now runs BrightStar, a franchise that helps aging boomers and seniors stay out of nursing homes and in their own houses by providing a full range of medical and nonmedical services.

Aileen, a baby boomer herself, hires nurses and certified nursing assistants who want to work full time or supplement their income.

"Boomers expect quality in their lives," Aileen said. "We shop at places like Nordstrom's, and we come to expect a certain standard. That includes healthcare."

A franchise with BrightStar in 2009 cost around $100,000 to $160,000. This includes a $35,000 franchise fee and frequently updated marketing materials. Also included is the company's proprietary cutting-edge Web-based management system that integrates personnel management, payroll and billing, and sales.

"I never in a million years thought I would be doing this," Aileen said. "This is a thriving business, and you can feel good about yourself at the end of the day. How great is that?"

Does an in-home healthcare career sound more interesting than retail? We thought so. Contact BrightStarHealthcare.com, Healthcare jobs.org, or MedHunting.com for a healthy alternative to your depressing, jobless lifestyle.

Companies that manufacture home healthcare products, such as walkers and wheelchairs, will be prospering in the next decade as well. This means there are factory, sales, and management jobs that will start popping up just as boomers' knees start giving out so get out there and create an opportunity for yourself before they put *you* into a home! QualityMedical Supplies.com and AllianceMedEquip.com (Alliance Medical Equipment & Respiratory Pharmacy Inc.) offer jobs in this "hip" industry.

As we've stressed in this chapter, boomers "do not go gentle into that good night." They will go kicking and screaming if they have anything to say about it. Boomers want to spend their last days in good health and comfort, so if you have a great idea for hot pink wheelchairs or zebra-print shower chairs, get it designed and hit the patent office like some of these other brilliant minds have done.

SharpBrains, a marketing firm that tracks mental health products, reports the U.S. brain fitness industry is predicted to exceed $2 billion by 2015. This tells you that boomers would rather play brain games than get Alzheimer's disease. (Researchers at the Johns Hopkins Bloomberg School of Public Health in Maryland say one in 85 people worldwide will have Alzheimer's by 2050.) Open your mind. Do a few brain squats and check out these places for stimulating careers in this new industry: VibrantBrains.com, SharpBrains.com, and PositScience.com.

Body and Soul

Boomers are obsessed with not only acting and thinking young but also looking young. They are fixated on external beauty, so here's your chance to capitalize on their vanity. Aging baby boomers are seeking out the Fountain of Youth more than ever. Whether it's to combat new wrinkles or to relax, these hipsters are rushing into day spas and destination spas. They are robbing their 401(k)s for facelifts and cheek implants—not those cheeks, *those* cheeks. Jobs as estheticians and careers in plastic surgeons' offices are as plentiful as the wrinkles on a boomer's face.

EstheticianJobs.com as well as SkinScienceInstitute.com are great places to start your search for a gig in a spa, hotel, resort, or doctor's office. If you previously worked as an administrative assistant or a receptionist before you were canned, and you're not bad looking, there are plastic surgeons that need front and back office help. In addition to a paycheck, the perks of Botox and silicon are great benefits. MedHunters.com and MedicalWorkers.com are two great sites to start your search for office jobs where you get to look at "before" and "after" pretty people all day.

Massage is yet another avenue that has become a hot seller. There are millions of boomers waiting for you to poke, prod, and knead them—all in the name of youth.

MassageEnvy.com and MassageFranchiseReview.com are two sites where you can find relaxing franchise opportunities. As for jobs as a masseuse that don't include a "happy ending," these sites are completely legitimate: StudyMassage.com/careers and AlternativeHealthBusiness.com.

Home Groovy Home

Now that boomers are being offered cool products that help them keep moving and in their houses, they want really cool homes. They don't want the last bed they sleep in to be in a smelly convalescent hospital with linoleum floors and a roommate that sounds as if he or she is coughing up a lung. Nope, they want a pad with 'tude—that's where a new job or career can come in for you!

Woodland Village, a 55-year-old-plus apartment complex, located in San Marcos, California, is just one example of the new housing being offered to boomers. The gated apartment community offers units with a variety of features typically found in single-family homes: nine-foot ceilings, washers and dryers, and solid maple cabinets in spacious kitchens. The grounds are green and lush, and extra-large swimming pools and gas barbecues are available for the tenants.

"It looks like as fine a hotel [as] you've ever been in," said developer Craig Engstrand. "Woodland Village is second to none." There also is a clubhouse with dancing, a movie theater, and a gym. Not to be overlooked is an espresso and wine bar.

According to a survey conducted by the AARP, when a rental housing option with luxury amenities is offered to active adults at a monthly after tax cost equivalent to home ownership, a significant number will choose to rent. The ability to free up liquidity when "downsizing" the household is attractive to many seniors. Places such as Woodland Village (WoodlandVillageApts.org) usually need recreation directors, cosmetologists, sales associates, and more.

So in the end, boomers will be great for the economy and job market until the last one is pushing up daisies. It's up to you to figure out how you're going to make money while creating a new life, a new job, and a new attitude for yourself. What are you waiting for? None of us is getting any younger!

CHAPTER ELEVEN

The Diverse Face of the Job Market

"Women now have choices. They can be married, not married, have a job, not have a job, be married with children, unmarried with children. Men have the same choice we've always had. Work or prison."

—Tim Allen

Here's the great news for everyone, whether you're female, male or somewhere in between: this may be the first time in history that you can benefit from an increasing number of women in a workforce once dominated by men. Why is this exciting? Because women are starting new businesses in record numbers. Back in 2008, when the recession was just getting started, female-driven businesses generated nearly $2 trillion in sales. While 81 percent of workers who got the ax were men, women-owned companies laid off fewer employees than male-owned firms. The Center for Women's Business Research reports that women now own more than 10 million companies. So, as more women gain skills and experience in fields that haven't yet been explored, new ideas evolve. More jobs are created. Everyone wins. Diversity in today's workforce is vital to reshaping businesses in the new economy, and that's good for everyone.

If you're a man, don't skip this chapter. Read with an open mind. You'll find out how women in the workplace can be an asset to you. We'll be talking about challenges, resources, and key success tips for women of all ages, but you'll benefit from this conversation as well. Having a successful woman as your ally will help you develop your accomplishments not only in the workforce but also in your personal life.

Gentlemen, you'll learn how to play with the big gals here. The benefits are great, if you go for it. Be a fly on the wall. This is your guide to building a winning team. Ladies, we want to help you find important insights on how to take your skills to the bank—and cash in. Whether you like to work with your hands, your brain, or your imagination, you'll learn about opportunities that can put you in the driver's seat. If the man in your life gets downsized (loses his job, that is), you might be the one your family counts on until he finds work again.

Your Control Panel

Before you evaluate what type of job or business suits your lifestyle, imagine your life as a pilot's control panel. There is a button for each kind of life stage in which you may find yourself. In fact, you may be in one or several of these life stages right now (and we're not talking midlife crisis, okay?). One thing may lead to another, but each one of the following situations has its unique set of challenges. Which one applies to you?

- Need a solid job with good pay and benefits?
- Entrepreneur?
- High-ranking executive or political leader?
- Pregnant, what now?
- Working mom or dad?
- Work at home?
- Parent reentering the workforce?
- Military personnel returning to civilian work?
- Broke and struggling, how do I survive?
- Over 50, am I over-the-hill?

This chapter will address the stages on this control panel and include some of the tools you can use to jump-start your career, business, or job search. And guys, listen up: some of these situations might apply to your life. Are you a single dad? Is your wife expecting? Will your girlfriend, sister, mother, or daughter be returning to school to find a new career?

We want to make sure we help your entire family out of the scary situation you might have found yourself in during this tough economy.

In a shrinking job market, women should explore fields that are considered "nontraditional," or populated mostly by men. Hopefully our society will reach a point in time where work is just work that any qualified person—male or female—can perform without any social stigma.

One example: Theresa, a former teacher, earned her pilot's license when she was a teenager. Her mother, who always regretted not having the opportunity to learn to soar, had encouraged Theresa to fly like her father and her grandfather. The young woman thought about flying as a career, but her school counselors, and even her own father, encouraged her to go to college and earn a teaching credential.

"My dad thought it was great that I had my wings, but he thought it was more of a hobby for me," Theresa said. "He thought it would be too difficult for me to make a living as a pilot because I was a woman. I agreed with him for a long time."

Theresa earned her bachelor's degree and became a high school history teacher, but after five years realized she had made a mistake.

"My heart wasn't in it, and I thought I was shortchanging the students," she said. "I was so unhappy that my relationship with my boyfriend was suffering. I took a leave of absence and flew on a cross-country trip in a Cherokee 6 [a small, single-engine airplane] by myself to think about what I wanted to do with my life. I think it took me about two hours to realize that by flying I was doing exactly what I was meant to do."

Theresa finished out the school year while taking advanced classes; she also obtained her basic ratings and even became a Certified Flight Instructor and Ground Instructor. She then said goodbye to her students and began job hunting. After a year of applying for airline jobs and being turned down, she realized the road to her goal was rough.

"I didn't want to think that my gender had anything to do with not finding a job, but I think it had *something* to do with it," she said. "There are of course many female pilots, but I think it's still considered a 'male' career. Gender discrimination in hiring is unlawful. Sure, the numbers of female pilots have increased, but they are still nowhere near 50 percent of the pilot population."

Theresa soon realized that she needed to become even more specialized if she wanted to fly for a living, so she took courses to become a helicopter pilot and earned her Commercial Rotorcraft License. Soon after she became certified, she landed a job as a pilot for a sightseeing company in Las Vegas. From there she moved up to executive transport and now works as a pilot for emergency medical services.

> *"I want them to know that it's not just lip service when someone says that if you really love to do something, then there is nothing, and I mean nothing, that can stop you!"*

"Flying a helicopter is so fantastic, but I still fly planes both professionally and for enjoyment," she said. "I am starting to speak at high school campuses across the country to spread the message to young women that it's not just the men who can fly planes, it's also about girl power. I want them to know that it's not just lip service when someone says that if you really love to do something, then there is nothing, and I mean *nothing*, that can stop you!"

Fly Girls Do it with the Guys

Do you know any women who dream of flying? Gals, if you want to fly like an eagle while earning a paycheck, there are plenty of places you can check out for career information. According to 2006 Federal Aviation Administration Airman data, women make up about 6 percent of the total number of pilots in the United States, or about 36,100 of 597,100 pilots. Of that, there are more than 7,200 with Commercial Pilot Certificates, and more than 5,000 with Airline Transport Pilot certificates.

If you're interested in taking this a step farther, you might want to look into flying helicopters. If that excites you, visit WhirlyGirls.org. This site has 1,570 Whirly-Girls members from 41 countries signed up and ready to answer questions. They can direct you to schools, loans, scholarships, and jobs so you can soar with the guys. One more thing. If you want to look skyward, the International Society of Women Airline Pilots (ISWAP) has even more information and aviation ideas at ISWAP.org; put them permanently on your radar.

According to studies compiled by Catalyst, the top think tank for women's workplace issues, more women are exploring "nontraditional" careers, but they are still a minority in high-level executive positions and leadership. Men are still a minority in education and service industries, so here's your chance, ladies, to even the playing field. Gentlemen, your chances of being hired by a woman will improve as they launch new businesses in nontraditional fields. Their company will benefit from your experience and expertise. And the men's room won't be so crowded.

Hot Jobs in the Skilled Trade Industry

Even if giant corporations are going bankrupt, the stuff our world is made of—cars, machines, buildings, and computers—still need to be built, maintained, and fixed when they break down. Skilled trade work—jobs like welders, carpenters, or machinists—is a wide open field. It's not sexy work. It's physical and dirty, which is kind of sexy now that we think of it! The pay ranges anywhere from $10 to $40 or more per hour, which is nothing to sneeze at. During the last recession that hit the United States—2002 to 2003—many industries were unable to find enough skilled laborers to fill job openings. We expect this may happen again.

Training and skill-building programs that prepare you for careers in technical trades such as computer programming are plentiful and are worthwhile investments. The National Association of Women in Construction (NAWiC.org) promotes and supports women in construction-related fields. Also, Wider Opportunities for Women (WOWonline. org), based in Washington, D.C., features a wide range of resources and programs.

Clean Up by Doing the Dirty Work

Girly-girl electricians, welders, green engineers, auto mechanics, truckers, and heavy equipment operators are all in high demand. The pay typically is higher than minimum wage. For example, welders make anywhere from $10 to $18 per hour for production work, and $18 to $28 per hour in the construction sector. Electricians and green engineers can potentially earn even more. Here's a closer look at the top trade industry jobs:

Welder—According to the American Welding Society, by 2010 there will be a shortage of more than 200,000 skilled welders in the U.S. workforce. When government money is poured into infrastructure and construction projects, there will be even more opportunities. The pay and benefits tend to be high, ranging from $10 to $28 per hour, with construction jobs on the higher end, so get out your *Flashdance* outfit and emote your inner Jennifer Beals.

Electrician—Broadband infrastructure is a high-growth area. As rural communities and urban buildings transition to the fastest technologies, wiring for computers and telecommunications equipment will be needed. An increase in power plant construction over the next 10 years will require a significant number of electricians as well. The pay is $16 to $27 an hour, with some specialized work garnering the biggest premiums.

Green engineer—As we mentioned in Chapter Four, with the push toward greening America's cities, there will be a slew of jobs in everything clean and green. Women with skills in construction, engineering, and architecture will be in high demand. Apollo Alliance, a coalition of environmental groups, politicians, and labor unions that focuses on renewable energy, says there will be three to five million more green jobs by 2018. There's a wide variety, from the installation and rotrofitting of water heaters and other energy-saving components in buildings, to solar panel and wind turbine installation, maintenance, and repair. Salaries start at $40,000, and, depending on skills and experience, many salaries run even higher.

Auto repair—The Car Care Council is seeing a growing demand for women in the auto repair field, and its Women's Board gives scholarships for training. Auto mechanics used to be almost all men, maybe because these jobs required heavy lifting and a lot of physical strength. But as vehicles have

(continued on the next page)

changed, so has the workforce. Many cars now have computer systems with electronic sensors, which require mechanics to understand technology, not wrenches. Average pay is around $15 per hour, and how hot will you look in those greasy jumpsuits?

Trucker—There has been a trucker shortage for years. Sure, those truck stops aren't too glamorous, but if more women were truckers, more people (like savvy businesswomen) would build them to better standards. Imagine if there were truck stops where a driver could grab a massage and a facial, have her nails done, and eat a healthy meal! A trucker's pay runs $13.33 to $21.04 an hour, about a quarter more than traditional women's jobs. Yet only about 5 percent of American drivers are female. If you can't deal with long hours alone on the road, consider becoming a light driver who picks up and delivers merchandise and packages within a certain area, or a route driver who delivers and sells a company's products over established routes.

Heavy equipment operator—Don't let the word *heavy* intimidate you. There's no lifting involved. You just have to know how to drive. Whether it's driving a forklift, digging utility trenches, or paving roads, equipment operators will have their pick of jobs in the new economy. The average pay is $14 to $24 per hour—and unionized workers earn even more. International Union of Operating Engineers and the Associated General Contractors of America apprentice programs offer three years of paid on-the-job training. Graduates usually have better job opportunities.

Training, Apprenticeships, and Job Placement in Construction-Related Fields

Newcomers to construction-related fields may have a tough time figuring out where the jobs are. Working with a construction staffing company will help you find work anywhere in the country. Visit these construction staffing companies to browse the possibilities. In their advance search boxes, enter "construction jobs" or "construction staffing." Kimmel & Associates recruits for general construction, mechanical contracting, electrical contracting, and more. Construction Intern, a sector of Kimmel & Associates, is a service devoted exclusively to internships within the construction industry. You can post your resume there to allow companies searching for interns in construction and engineering to find you.

Women—and the men rooting for their success—should check out Hard Hatted Women (HardHattedWomen.com). This site offers job listings, training programs, information, and support for women in construction or those who want to enter construction-related fields.

It's no secret that women who have complicated lives often accomplish extraordinary things. When Shelley's husband was laid off from his construction job in Denver, they had less than $40 in the bank, three young kids, and bills that were due. Shelley tells the story of how she became an award-winning construction contractor:

"My husband knew the construction industry as an employee but had never run a business in his life," she said. "I had some basic education on business and marketing. Since most of my life had involved my being a self-employed musician, photographer, and artist, I had business sense, but not in construction! I didn't know the difference between a Phillips head screw and a hex head.

"My first move was creating a unique name and logo for the new company. Men that I had to deal with made fun of the name, Dancing River Construction, when they were using names like Smith Brothers Construction. They were none too pleased to have my feminine approach to the field coming onto their turf. Our motto, 'When Honey-Do Becomes Honey-Won't, Call Dancing River Construction,' could be heard all over Denver.

"I decided that the only way I was going to learn this business and succeed was to be totally honest about my ignorance. I went through many suppliers and subcontractors who simply refused to deal with me, and yet there were others who appreciated my honesty and eagerness to learn the ropes. One of the most difficult aspects of being a woman in the construction industry is having mostly men around you nonstop and having to totally

> *"I decided that the only way I was going to learn this business and succeed was to be totally honest about my ignorance."*

change your style of communicating. If something went wrong on a job site or with one of my employees, I had to take a very tough stance and mean business, which was a challenge at times. Because of my professionalism, a level of mutual respect was gained between us all.

"My unconventional approach worked to grow our own business, but it also benefited the very men who, in the beginning, literally laughed at my business name and marketing approaches. Women became my biggest customers because they valued the fact that they were hiring a company led by a woman—which meant they had a woman to talk to about designing a great kitchen or bathroom. I was eventually appointed to the National Home Builder's Association Board of Directors for the Remodelers Council. Very few women had been invited to join that group, let alone be chosen on the national board, so that was quite an accomplishment. At my speaking engagements, especially those aimed at young women, I reminded them that 'if a woman with no experience in an industry can make it to the top, so can you!'"

Desk Jobs and Brain Power Equal Big Opportunity and Bigger Money: Women Engineers in Demand

Why is it profitable for women to study engineering and science and not home economics? Demographics have shifted. The demand for engineers is on the rise as aging baby boomers approach retirement and there aren't enough college graduates to replace them. The talent pool is swiftly drying up.

Engineering is the skill that puts scientific knowledge to practical use everywhere from construction to product design, technology, and more. Today's women just might become tomorrow's heroes if they can save the country from falling behind the rest of the world and maintain the status of global preeminence and leadership. The bottom line in engineering is, there simply aren't enough *people* (male or female) who are qualified to fill the jobs.

Does engineering sound boring? Think again. When you comingle engineering with art and design, it becomes a powerful and practical form of creative expression. With a girl-friendly engineering degree you can design bridges or bras, semiconductors or shoes. Female-friendly programs designed to attract women are emerging to address both sides of your brain.

Will there really be huge opportunities for women in construction and engineering? Let's put it this way—America's infrastructure is a mess, and it needs to be fixed. The American Society of Civil Engineers (ASCE) gave our infrastructure a "D" on a report card that assessed the condition and capacity of the country's public works. ASCE reports that nearly one in four of the nation's 600,000 bridges are structurally deficient or functionally obsolete. Remember those news stories? Bridges are caving in and collapsing. The number of dams deemed unsafe has risen by more than 33 percent in the last 10 years. Flash back to the levee that broke and wiped out New Orleans after Hurricane Katrina. Let's talk railroad tracks. Have you been on a train lately? It's a rough, rickety ride compared to the swift, high-speed rails of Europe and Japan. ASCE also reports that railroads are investing about $2 billion annually on repairs and maintenance just trying to hold that mess together. All those repairs mean slower freight and higher costs of the products that are shipped by rail. Roads aren't much better. About 34 percent of America's major roads are in bad condition, and 36 percent of the major urban roads are congested—both adding to the nearly 43,000 traffic fatalities each year. Oh, and did we mention the country got poor grades for conditions in aviation, schools, solid waste, transit, drinking water, wastewater, hazardous waste, parks and recreation, and ports and navigable waterways?

Yes, the United States needs a makeover, a facelift, and a major overhaul. Really. Most of these systems were built in the nineteenth- and twentieth-century industrial age, and they're reaching their limits. ASCE estimates that $1.6 trillion would be needed over five years to bring our infrastructure to good condition.

In June 2009, President Barack Obama pledged a $787 billion stimulus package to create jobs, increase spending on maintenance projects at military bases, fund about 1,600 road and airport projects, hire approximately 135,000 teachers and other school staffers, and establish 125,000 summer jobs for youth under the supervision of the Department of Labor. Consider finding out what it takes to get involved in the overhaul, in any capacity. Skills you had from your previous job might be transferable to related industries.

Be on the lookout for jobs at new and innovative companies that invest in developing and commercializing technology-based solutions to some of the U.S. infrastructure issues.

New Industries on the Horizon

As women contribute to new technologies, they'll help expand those markets. Thousands of other jobs that propel them, such as contracting, sales, marketing, and customer service, will burgeon. One new technology—solar power—is on the verge of changing the world. The National Academy of Engineering predicts that in theory it will be possible to have solar power up and running sufficiently to meet everyone's energy needs within 20 years. They predict that sunlight can be turned into electricity using thin sheets of plastic with energy-converting semiconductors printed on them in nano-ink. Wow—plastic sheets that generate more energy than smokestacks.

Art and Politics

Want a serving of politics with your science and art? "They" want you to have it. New holistic programs envision you not only as tomorrow's engineers but also as future global leaders. There are now special courses being offered on politics and leadership so you can navigate a political system and get the inside track to having your ideas approved, funded, and out there. Need a creative outlet? Here's a fun Web site for provocative and political female artists. You can make connections; post your ideas, artwork, and links to your blog at FemalePersuasion.net. Guys, extraordinary women have connections. Go ahead and network. Give her your card; she may help you find a job.

Does Fox News have you craving to become an original thinker so you can dive into art, politics, and truth telling to help people understand the complicated issues facing the nation? Do you thirst to become a political writer or actor, or do you want to create satirical plays? Then try out for the San Francisco Mime Troupe at SFMT.org, or channel your political angst by joining the Living Theatre (LivingTheatre.org) in New York City. Political satire is big business for both men and women, and if you don't believe us, check out the popularity of *The Daily Show* and *The Colbert Report*. Who's laughing now?

Women Can Do This!

What do you want to be when you grow up? Maybe engineering, science, and construction aren't the first things that come to a girl's mind when she's asked that question. But according to a panel discussion sponsored by L'Oreal USA to encourage emerging female talent in the science, technology, engineering, and mathematics (STEM) fields, girls are perfect for learning and becoming masters of the craft:

Girls mature earlier—they can move faster into advanced classes.

Girls are less competitive and, because they can think outside the box, they can be more innovative.

Girls are predisposed to do things that help people; hence, engineering, technology, and science are natural choices, if they see it as helping people.

Girls are more practical—another reason STEM professions are a natural fit.

Engaging women in engineering and science engages the diversity of women's unique—and untapped—perspectives.

For smart chicks who want high-paying, recession-proof jobs in science, technology, engineering and mathematics fields, check out:

Anita Borg Institute for Women and Technology at AnitaBorg.org, which connects women and technology.

Association for Women in Science—AWIS.org—provides information about internships, scholarships, volunteer opportunities, and job listings.

National Center for Women in Information Technology, Mentor Net, and the E-Mentoring Network for Diversity in Engineering and Science can also turn you into a money-making geek. The latter site connects protégés from colleges and universities and mentors from industry, government, and higher education on one-on-one, e-mail-based mentoring relationships connecting the whole nerd world.

Support for Executives and Businesswomen

Each year, more groundwork is built for the up-and-coming leaders of tomorrow.

"[Eighty] million cracks were made in the glass ceiling," Secretary of State Hillary Clinton said in a letter to her supporters in 2008, summing up her bold race for president, her political career, and what it means for women to move into ranks of leadership.

Change is on the horizon. And there's hope for men who dream of being a stay-at-home dad while the wife is at her high-powered job. Or, if you're both power players, the two of you can buy that island sooner than you imagined. Some people love to run the show. For others, it's a burden and a headache. Not all men love the rat race, and not all women love taking the kids to soccer games. Some people really want to stay home, run a household, and be present in their children's daily lives. Others need to be out of the house taking on challenges. As the job markets shift to a more balanced distribution of the sexes, men and women will have more lifestyle choices.

Take Advantage of a Failing Situation

Changing times means expanding opportunities for women and savvy men who capitalize on this trend. As companies face serious problems in regard to their bottom line, the more open they are to try solutions they haven't tried before. You can seize the opportunity to be a hero and prove you can make a difference. Companies might be willing to take a chance on someone who can solve their problems, especially with success models like the Principal Group, where 50 percent of the most senior positions are held by women. Principal is doing well. This Des Moines–based insurance/financial company has been one of the most female-friendly workplaces in America since 1966, when it offered part-time hours and summers off. In 1974, the company introduced flexible work schedules before the practice became trendy. In conditions that supported women's needs, women were able to perform incredibly well and boost the company's bottom line.

To get an idea where the waters are warm, visit WorkingMother .com to find out which are the 100 most female-friendly companies and law firms.

In spite of the layoffs, the insurance business has job openings. People still have to insure their cars, health, and life. Selling insurance isn't for everyone, but if you have an entrepreneurial streak, it can be very lucrative and flexible with residual income. Even if you have no desire to be in the insurance/financial business, Principal offers free help and career advice once a month via a teleclass to further the needs of businesswomen. The teleclass features an exciting topic like "The Five Secrets of Millionaire Business Women" and an interview with a successful female CEO who shares her experiences and tips. To see their monthly program schedule and register for a free teleclass, visit Principal.com. In the advance search box, enter "free teleclass for women." Strength is gathered in numbers. Seek out blogs and sites with job boards, news sharing, and tips. Here are some sites where you can be part of women pulling together to push for that tipping point:

- The Glass Hammer (GlassHammer.com) is an online community designed for women executives in financial services, law, and business. At this site you can share experiences, network, and browse job listings.
- The Thin Pink Line (TheThinPinkLine.com) is a blog that is coauthored by four savvy businesswomen who share what they've learned along the way with regard to jobs and family life.

Here are some helpful sites that support both men and women who have been laid off:

- Laid Off and Looking (Blogs.WSJ.com/laidoff/) is a great site to check out as well. The Wall Street Journal blog follows eight out-of-work MBAs as they search for jobs in a post-meltdown world.
- The 405 Club (The405Club.com) is a site established by recently unemployed, highly educated people that serves as a place for newbies and sages alike to commiserate and to find and share new tips and tricks that will help navigate this tough environment.

Sneaking Through the Side Door

If you're finding it hard to get hired into a large company directly, try offering your expertise to them on a consulting basis. We know starting from scratch can be a bitch. No pun intended. Volunteering for a nonprofit is an excellent way to establish credibility and a track record. Because most of these organizations desperately need you, it's an awesome place to show off your talents, make a difference, and get glowing testimonials. Credibility equals clients and flexible hours.

Jeff was an out-of-work cinematographer who founded a charity for homeless teens in Los Angeles, California. He told us: "After I received my nonprofit status, I invited several women I met at a support group for unemployed entertainment professionals to form an advisory board. Their impressive credits attracted celebrities, and the organization became a well-known source for talent. Eventually my board members landed lucrative positions with Fortune 500 companies, and I invited new people who were out of work to volunteer for the organization." Jeff's nonprofit continues to be a launchpad for unemployed executives who want to stay involved in the community and showcase their skills.

Help for Entrepreneurs

When it comes to cottage industries, they are great places to be a big fish in a small pond. An increasing number of women who have been laid off or downsized while they were climbing the corporate ladder are going out and grabbing their own ladders. Business executive service companies contract to several companies on retainer or per project basis. If you were laid off, and you were working in upper management of the banking industry, try offering your skills as an independent controller. (See the next chapter for more freelancing information and ideas.)

Looking back in history, cottage industries proliferated during recessions when downsized employees needed to create some kind of certainty for themselves. According to statistics reported by Catalyst, most small businesses and an increasing trend of start-ups are owned by women. But with the credit crunch, how do you start up and get your business rolling?

Using today's resources, you can start a business with very little money. As a result of so many women pulling together to make conditions viable for success, you can learn about financing and business skills, and get advice on how to run the show. For a taste of what's possible, visit Springboard Enterprises (Springboard.org).

Springboard is a huge support organization that offers access to funding, venture capital, and mentoring programs to help start women in business. They connect women entrepreneurs and investors both nationally and globally. Springboard educates, showcases, and supports you while you seek out capital and build your businesses. Cool beans!

Political Leaders Can Wear Lipstick

Are you a people person? More women are running for positions in government office. For information on how to run a political campaign, visit the League of Women Voters (LWV.org) and EMILY's List (EMILYsList .org)—these chicks helped put a president in the White House.

Help for Working Moms

Pregnant? No problem. Graduate programs offer childbirth, parental, and family leave to help women pursue academic goals, and accommodate changing family circumstances. Sure, for women, doing anything a man can do is easy. But on top of all that, they have to deal with that bump in the road—pregnancy—child bearing, and breastfeeding. Expectant mothers have to exit the workforce for, at the very least, the amount of time it takes for prenatal care, delivery, and recovery. And now . . . the double whammy. If the other wage earner in the house loses his job, what are the options? Mothers are more likely than fathers to work part time or take leave when the baby is born. When faced with the high cost of child care, a couple might decide that the lower wage earner should stay home—or not immediately seek to reenter the workforce after a layoff, when the economy is bad. On the bright side, if both of you end up unemployed and home together with the kids, you'll have more family time than you ever dreamed of and a chance to work on different strategies with your mate.

Women, if you're laid off while pregnant, parenting small children, or returning to work after having children, you may need some coaching in addition to thinking outside the box. Career consulting and help for professional women to find better ways to blend work and family can be found at sites like MomsAndJobs.com. Founder Nancy Collamer is an online career expert for big sites such as Oprah Winfrey's Oxygen and ClubMom.com.

Collamer offers private coaching to show you how to navigate a full range of "back-to-work strategies." The site has a career center with links you can use to post your resume and templates to build a career profile. Moms and Jobs also offers listings of family-friendly companies, flexible jobs (telecommuting, job-share, part-time, flextime, etc.), contract, freelance, and temporary opportunities and work-at-home options suitable for professional-level women. Employers and recruiters can post and search on the site.

At JobsAndMoms.com, you can download a "Back to Work Toolkit" for a reasonable price. It's a 91-page guide that's written for professional moms who want to return to paid employment (or entrepreneurship) and is filled with ideas that are specific, detailed, and simple to implement.

Tools for Struggling Single Parents

Financial survival is an ongoing battle for single parents who lack support and have lost their livelihoods. Money matters and practical financial planning are almost impossible to figure out if you're not an economics ninja. To see how much it costs to live in your city and what you need to make for ends to meet, try the Self Sufficiency Calculator (TheCalculator.org).

This online calculator is based on the Self Sufficiency Standard, which measures how much income is needed for a family of a given composition—one-person household to large family size—in a given place, to adequately meet its basic needs without any public or private assistance.

This free online tool does the following:

- Shows you what hourly wage you have to make to support yourself or your family, based on where you live.
- Tells you what you and/or your family should be making based on market value prices for rent, food, healthcare, transportation, taxes, child care, and miscellaneous expenses.
- Allows you to test different work or living options and see how these affect your bottom line.
- Develop career planning goals so you can work toward a better paying job.

Military Personnel Returning to Work

Coming home from active duty to a nation with one of the highest unemployment rates in history sucks. You don't have to go it alone. You can grab some advice from dedicated groups who are all about servicemen and women in transition. The Business and Professional Women (BPW) site found at BPWUSA.org, is where female veterans can post a resume and get legal support and career advice, especially about military transitioning, and Vet Jobs (VetJobs.com) is available to all members of the United States military. These sites list companies with human resource departments that are well versed in veterans' benefits, continuing education reimbursement, career counseling or planning services. Even more beneficial to military families, BPWUSA has a program called "Women Joining Forces—Closing Ranks, Opening Doors," which supports women veterans as they transition from military to civilian life.

Quick Cash

Michelle, an administrative assistant who was bouncing from job to job, could never stay employed long enough to be eligible for unemployment benefits. "I decided to get a degree in mathematics when I heard that mathematicians and actuaries are in demand. It's a six-figure salary, and the work environment is low stress." She qualified for a student loan with a cosigner. But she had to get some cash flow going while taking courses toward a degree online. "I started freelancing as a bill collector," Michelle said. "With so many defaults on car loans, credit cards, and mortgages, I found plenty of openings for bill collectors. I have to deal with a lot of angry phone conversations, but so what? I've been doing that for *years* with my ex-husband."

"Aim high, and you won't shoot your foot off."

Check out jobs with organizations that flourish in economic downturns, such as crisis management companies, universities, career services providers, and law firms that specialize in bankruptcy.

Tough times call for creative measures. No matter what your comfort zone was, branch out, find a mentor, and apply your unique abilities to something you have never considered. Talk to women who took a chance. Phyllis Diller, one of the first female comedians to work in a male-dominated field, once said, "Aim high, and you won't shoot your foot off."

CHAPTER TWELVE

An Endless Summer:
INDEPENDENTS AND FREELANCERS

*"I'd be hanging out in my bathrobe all day, stinky, just
writing, and my mom allowed me to do this—
as long as I was writing songs. She said, 'As long
as you're seriously working on music, I'll support you. Don't
get a job, because if you work, it will crush you."*

—*Rufus Wainwright*

Have you been kicked-to-the-curb by corporate America? Handed your walking papers from Wall Street? Given the boot by your boss? Well, if you take our advice, it could be the last time you will ever lose a job again.

In this chapter you will learn how to become your own boss. That's right, no jerk telling you what to do or when to do it—unless you're in the habit of talking to yourself quite severely, and we can't help you there.

Because both authors, Kitty Martini and Candice Reed, have worked successfully for themselves, this chapter should be very informative and helpful to those who want to become independent contractors or freelancers.

So here's what we're going to do:

- Assist you in determinging whether you have what it takes to successfully work at home. We want you to examine your ability to work without much social interaction and decide if you're assertive enough to sell your product or service all by your lonesome. We want you to be able to really figure out if you have what it takes to work for yourself. (It's okay; not everyone can do it.)

- Help you find out what talents you have that can earn you money without going back to work for someone else.
- Teach you how to find and actually get paid from clients.
- Give dos and don'ts of working for yourself, including socking money away during the good times for downturns in the economy and how to keep you from becoming distracted and not completing your work.
- Show you how to avoid going to jail for tax evasion.

So let's get started. The safety net of putting on a suit and driving to a really tall building and getting in the elevator with 20 strangers may be what you crave in life. You need this day-to-day routine. But, if you've taken your head out of the sand for any extended period of time lately, you have seen a very scary job market out there.

As we keep saying in this book, you have to become creative to thrive in this new economy. It's a tough world out there, but you can, and you will, survive. We're not promising that by working for yourself you will be a gazillionaire, because that is so old school. We want you to find a creative way to make a nice living, pay the mortgage, buy a cool car every five years, take a few vacations—you know, live a nice life in moderation. (We understand if this all is a new concept, but get used to it; it's the twenty-first century!)

Let's move forward and see if there is something that will make you happy and make you money.

"Getting fired redefined my life," said Issa. "In a sense, you could sum up my experience by saying, 'I'm a corporate high tech couch potato manager turned internationally known fire dancing instructor and artist.' I left my corporate job as the dot-com was beginning to crumble in the Bay Area. My life was woefully out of balance: all work, no play. And I was trying desperately to integrate my alternative living ideals—late night dancing and Burning Man thinking—into my corporate world. When I wore glitter to work and my VP pulled me into his office and said,

"I'm a corporate high tech couch potato manager turned internationally known fire dancing instructor and artist."

'You'll never get ahead in this company wearing glitter to work,' I knew change needed to happen. Through a series of unexpected events, I ended up starting the world's premier poi fire dancing school. I can confidently say I've changed the face of the art form on the West Coast of the United States."

Working for *You*

Did you know that the word *boss* comes from the Dutch word *baas*, which historically means "master"? As in slave driver. Nice, right? Well, if you finally want to stop kissing boss (*baas*) butt and punching a time clock, the time is right to become self-employed. We're not talking about finding a job from a poster on a telephone pole or buying into a pyramid or multi-level scheme ("Work from home and make $10,000 a week!"). We are talking about figuring out what you have to offer and how to sell yourself. Ways to stop sending out your resume along with the rest of the herd. How to become an independent contractor. Independent contractors earn their livelihoods from their own businesses instead of depending upon the nine-to-five routine to earn a living. They are also referred to as consultants, freelancers, self-employed, entrepreneurs, and business owners—as well as "bums" by their moms . . . until the money starts coming in.

"I needed a new plan. I needed to be proactive because I was slowly going broke."

Taylor worked as a hair stylist at a high-end salon in Las Vegas where a haircut was almost $100. When the economy was cruising along, she was making more money than she knew what to do with, taking trips and buying clothes she didn't need. "At the end of each year I owed the IRS thousands of dollars," she said. "But it was cool because I had made so much."

Then the economy started to slow. "My clients began to go longer and longer without coming in, and then some started to disappear altogether. I still had to pay a pretty steep price for my booth, and it was getting harder and harder to pay the rent on my condo. I have to admit that I didn't put much away because I figured that people would always want haircuts." On some days Taylor would wait for a walk-in and only have two or three clients. "I needed a new plan. I needed to be proactive because I was slowly going broke."

The cosmetologist decided to e-mail all her friends and family, offering discount haircuts and color. Then she posted a notice on Craigslist and in her local free newspaper. Soon she was so busy that she quit the salon and bought a sink and other supplies and put them in her spare bedroom. "I realized one day that I was almost making the same amount of money that I used to make," she said. "Yes, I was working harder, but my clients appreciated the fact that they weren't getting ripped off. I'm much happier running my own business and still doing what I love to do."

Get a (Freelance) Life!

When you take the big step of becoming self-employed, you will find yourself typically working for a number of different clients and tackling projects that require different sets of skills that you have stored in your brain. Don't hold back on your creativity here. You may be afraid to take a risk. Scared that you don't have any real value or talents to offer others. Frightened of succeeding in this crazy world. We know you have the ability, service, and ingenuity, and people will gladly pay you for it. There's only one thing that prevents you from seeing this truth—fear of the unknown (cue: scary music).

We believe that all you really need is the courage to be yourself. Your real value is rooted in who you are, not what you do. Your biggest challenge is to figure out in that brainwashed corporate noggin of yours how to express your real self to the world. You may have been told all sorts of lies as to why you can't do what you've been dreaming all along. But you'll never know true happiness and fulfillment until you summon the courage to do it. So put down your ideas on paper and let it stew. While you await the muse to whisper encouraging words in your ear, let us toss a little reality your way.

So, what do you want to hear first? The good news or the bad news about being self-employed?

Let's start with the bad:

- You won't have job security.
- You might not get paid.
- You must pay self-employment taxes.
- You may be personally liable for business debts.
- You have no employer-provided benefits.

Damn! So what's the good news? Other than you've been set free? That you are now a free-range worker? That every ounce of time is now yours and yours alone?

- You are your own boss.
- You may very well be paid more than those nine-to-five worker bees.
- No federal or state tax is withheld from your pay.
- You can take a lot of increased business deductions.
- You can work anywhere you wish. You also may work in your pajamas or less, if you wish.
- You will be happier with your work—and in time happier with your life.

Okay, then, that last one trumps all the negative vibes we threw at you, so read on.

Before You Meet Your Muse

To find out more about the nuts and bolts of becoming an independent contractor or freelancer, here are some helpful sites:

GoFreelance.com
HomeBusiness.about.com
NASE.org (The National Association for the Self-Employed)
Nolo.com
Business.gov
MagentaCircle.ning.com

The key to a successful freelance career is routine. You need to give yourself a strict schedule, just like any job. People may complain about the inconvenience of the traditional situation—getting out of bed at the crack of dawn, dealing with the traffic, and putting in face time with coworkers—but that keeps most people honest and productive. Without a "normal" work routine, you may find yourself playing tennis for much of the day or lounging around the pool—which is okay if you have a BlackBerry and sunscreen.

It's important to remember that sometimes people with "real" jobs don't understand how much work it is just getting through the day, probably because they can't grasp the concept of working only for themselves. They can't even fathom it. They ask things like, "So, what did you do today?" and you reply that you spent five hours e-mailing and another two researching on the Internet, and a few hours on the phone. They in turn, may look at you like you're on permanent vacation, but when the checks start arriving, they'll figure it out. You have a job, but you work from home. We hate to belabor the point: not everyone is cut out for this life because you need to stay focused, be part salesperson and part creative director, and have a pretty darn good work ethic if you want to pay the bills.

Before You Take the Plunge

Before you give those Gucci suits to Goodwill Industries and jump into the field of freelancing and sweatpants, you need to look at all the positive aspects and the possible trade-offs you may make in terms of income, time, and security. Ask yourself these three important questions before you run out of unemployment benefits, before you blow what's left in your 401(k), and before you set off as a consultant/independent contractor/freelancer.

1. *Can you work alone?* Sometimes it's lonely when you first start working all . . . by . . . yourself. There are no coworkers to hang out with. No office parties and no drunken happy hours with staff. You also might take a lot of crap from loved ones. In the beginning, when you are struggling, family members may find it hard to sympathize with people such as yourself who work in their pajamas. You may make other friends who are self-employed, and if your business takes off, you may even eventually have to hire help, but that's probably down the line a bit. Just be sure you like spending time with yourself and by yourself and you can do it without a bottle of Jack Daniels.

2. *Can you afford to live the life of an independent contractor?* If you have thousands of dollars put aside to live on as you make your way in the world of the self-employed, then good for you. Quit looking for a corporate job and make the plunge. If you don't have the cash, be wary. You'll definitely need your own office, a computer, and a backup computer in case one is in the shop. You'll need extra phone lines, business cards, and other equipment it takes to run a small company. Then you have to anticipate that the checks will be trickling in slowly. Make sure you are okay living below the poverty line in the beginning. Trust us, it will be worth it when you are in Hawaii on a working vacation, fielding calls from clients while wearing a Speedo and sipping your piña colada.

3. *Can you be your own boss?* You get to decide when to work and when to head to lunch with your pals, but you also are only the one motivating yourself to make money. No one is going to tell you not to go shopping or to the ballgame instead of making a deadline or calling a client. It's all on your shoulders. Nobody else is going to come into your office and hand you an assignment. Only you can bring in the paycheck. Are you up to the task of being your own boss?

You might be wondering what you have to offer the world. Maybe you've been stuck in an office with no windows your whole working life and you can't begin to think of what you could do to earn a living now that you're out on the street. So let's brainstorm.

If you were a big shot, a middle manager (what does that title mean, anyway?), or even a worker drone with years of experience, you most likely can become a consultant. You can do what you were doing before, but now do it on your own terms.

Here are a few Web sites to get you thinking as a consultant: PowerHomeBiz.com and CareerOverview.com. At these places you can find articles, tips, and success stories to help you succeed in your new at-home venture.

Do You Have What It Takes?

Take this quick quiz to see if you have the right stuff to work for yourself:

- Do you consider yourself proactive?
- Do you enjoy taking risks?
- Are you resourceful—coming up with creative, imaginative ways to solve problems?
- Can you juggle many projects or responsibilities at one time?
- Do you adapt well to new situations and change?
- Are you continually trying to find answers to resolve an issue?
- Are you self-motivated, taking the initiative to complete projects without being requested?
- Do you want to be your own boss?

If you answered most of these questions with a resounding "Hell, yeah!" then you can work at home.

Or maybe you have a creative side, and business is just what you did to make your parents happy after you graduated from college. You could think about the self-help industry: people want to improve their lives in every aspect. Not only that, but there are a lot of depressed people walking around who need—no, *want*—someone to talk to. Potential freelance business ideas include family therapist, time management consultant, and personal development coach.

Web sites such as BLS.gov (The Bureau of Labor Statistics) and FreelanceSprout.com offer you ideas that you can apply to real life and help the poor, mentally unstable folks out . . . for a price. Here are some:

- *Business/career/freelance ideas:* Custom blog designer, college application consultant, or an Internet business plan writer are just some ideas. Check out EducationalConsulting.org and SahelTech.com to jump-start your exploration in these areas.
- *Health and wellness:* From diets to niche disease support groups, the Web has millions of ideas for careers in this

arena. Freelance businesses you can start: personal trainer, custom menu/grocery shopping developer, and weight loss coach. Exercise.about.com and ConsultantJournal.com will give you plenty to ponder.

- *Skills training:* You have the degree—consider that freelance teaching is becoming a viable marketplace. You can be a freelance math tutor, singing or voice instructor, freelance athletic coach, or foreign language instructor. Give yourself an A+ by checking out sites such as TutoringExchange.com and ALCInc.com (AllWorld Language Consultants Inc.).

- If you are a writer, you can make money by selling your thoughts and words. Books to purchase, or check out from the library if the unemployment checks are late, include: *Starting Your Career as a Freelance Writer* by Moira Anderson Allen, *The Greatest Freelance Writing Tips in the World* by Linda Jones and, better yet, buy author Candice Reed's e-Book, *Everyone's a Writer—The Real Truth Behind the Careers of Successful Freelance Journalists* from our Web site, ThankYouForFiringMe.org. Not everyone can be a writer, but maybe you have it in you and you just don't know it.

Sue developed Parkinson's disease while getting her master's degree in biomedical sciences. She found employment with a medical company, but she had numerous surgeries over the years, which made work difficult. Eventually her employer transferred her to a position for which she had little training.

> *"No matter how challenging my health is, I can maintain my freelance writing career, and I love what I do every day."*

"I could see that this was an effort to slowly squeeze me out of the company," Sue said. Soon afterward, she was fired. Sue found various temporary jobs, but it became apparent that work was causing her to have more medical troubles. She requested and received an early retirement, but knew she had more to offer and wasn't ready to quit on life.

"Because I studied journalism in college I wanted to use that experience somehow," she said. "Now I'm a freelance journalist for a local paper covering city hall, and I have seen my byline in many magazines. I have the flexibility I need. And I feel blessed that I had a second chance. No matter how challenging my health is, I can maintain my freelance writing career, and I love what I do every day."

Freelance for All and All for Freelancing!

But freelancing isn't only for artistic types. The fitness industry is ripe with opportunities to go on your own.

After starting out as a personal trainer at chain gyms like 24 Hour Fitness and L.A. Fitness, 30-year-old Ryan opened his own personal training business six years ago and hasn't looked back since. "The big gyms charge personal training clients up to $60 for a one-hour session, but I only made $16 per hour," Ryan said. "This way, I keep all the income and control my overhead, plus the taxes aren't as high." He took his time searching for lease space and found an affordable storefront only two blocks from the beach in Oceanside, California. Most of his equipment was purchased one piece at a time with saved-up cash earned from part-time jobs, although he did take out one $4,000 loan, cosigned by his parents to secure a good interest rate, to purchase a couple of large items. The loan has since been paid off, and he has never charged a business expense to a credit card.

Ryan's gym, Results Fitness, is a far cry from 24 Hour Fitness, with only two 10-foot by 20-foot modestly equipped studios . . . and that's exactly how he wants it. "Large gyms are overwhelming to many people," he said, "Especially retirees and people who suffer from obesity, physical and mental handicaps, and chronic health problems. Clients would ask if I could meet them at their homes instead of at the gym, and I soon realized there was a big demand for privacy," he said. His strategy of targeting special-needs clients differs from the traditional personal training target market of young clients with short-term weight loss goals. "Finding a way to stand out from the crowd is key," he said. "Plenty of trainers have figured out you can make a lot more money doing it on your own." Clients with chronic health problems also provide better financial stability because they are usually more mature and have long-term goals.

They also provide a greater sense of accomplishment for Ryan, who said helping people motivates him more than income.

Ryan is also free to recommend a protocol based on what he feels is best for the client, not company sales quotas. "I hated selling supplements at the gym, making a quota to keep my job, when I didn't even believe they helped the client," he said. "In fact, I hated it so much I basically didn't do it, and it definitely added fuel to the fire, motivating me even more to go out on my own." He supplements his income by renting his second studio to other personal trainers who want to test the self-employment waters without investing in their own gyms. "Working for yourself allows you the freedom to run your business how you see fit, with your own values," Ryan said.

Open for Business

Here we go. Excited? We are, now that you've figured out what you want to do with your second chance. You've pawned the family jewels to buy a new computer and purchase business cards—now what? Before you blow the last of your start-up money, let's go over a few things you don't need.

You don't need to set up a corporation. Go to city hall and apply for a business license, if it makes you feel important, but most small businesses are sole proprietorships, and they do just fine without one. You don't need a separate business checking account right away, if you don't want to pay a monthly fee. Some banks offer free checking, so shop around. You'll need some basic bookkeeping software for keeping track of business such as QuickBooks or QuickBooks online, and you should set up a PayPal account (PayPal.com) to make it easy for clients to pay you via electronic check, credit card, or money transfer. PayPal also has an invoicing feature, which makes billing and collecting a breeze. Most of your clients will be more than willing to pay you electronically. At the end of the year, they'll send you W-9 tax documents for filing with the IRS. If you can afford a bookkeeper, the service is well worth not having the headache of trying to figure out where you stand financially. Bookkeeping services are not as expensive as you would imagine. (It's a great freelance business as well.) Have a tax service or Certified Public Accountant do your income tax filing so you don't screw up with Uncle Sam. All these expenses are tax deductible.

You can build your own Web site with some of the many free templates offered on the Web from Yahoo Small Business, Go Daddy, or Homestead.

Here's something that might make a corporate ex-stooge like yourself go pale: don't write a business plan. Yes, that's what we said. You don't need pie charts and complicated goals. You are now in the creativity zone. Instead of a business plan, try a simple production schedule with a list of all the details that need to be handled by when. When you're starting out as a freelancer, over-thinking your plan can lead to anxiety and self-doubt. But if you can't sleep at night without a formal business plan, check out sites such as ContractedWork.com and AllFreelance.com.

Overall, don't spend time on tasks that won't make a difference to your bottom line. What is most important is getting the word out about your newfound business. After you cement your idea, and you buy your pens and build a snazzy Web site with PayPal, selling is the most important thing to be doing.

Show Me the Money

Often people with a creative streak have a hard time negotiating fees and handling payment issues. Lucky for you if your last job was in finance or the mortgage industry, and you know all the tricks of squeezing money out of people. But if you weren't born with a calculator in your brain stem, here are a few things to remember when negotiating the deal.

One way to assure there are no misunderstandings in regard to payment is to always discuss the terms up-front and get them in writing. You will be amazed at how many people think that now that you have become "artistic" you should give them your services for free. But for God's sake, don't; you'll make the rest of us look bad.

Getting a written contract or even an e-mail confirmation for a project is very important. You can even insist on an up-front payment before beginning any work. A signed contract and any other paperwork you can produce are always a help if you face collection problems, although most of the time, when the check is late, it's due to an invoice falling through the cracks in the accounting department.

Working for yourself typically means you don't have a set "payday," and you can rarely expect to make the same amount each week. You'll spend a lot of time hanging out with the mail deliverer and may even learn to recognize the sound of your mailbox opening from two miles away. This sporadically received income is all the more reason to keep a close eye on your finances. Each time you receive a payment from a client, record it in a notebook, spreadsheet, or bookkeeping software. You'll want to know the date the payment was received and the amount; if there were fees associated with receiving the payment, record those as well.

It's also a good idea to save 15 to 20 percent of all income for taxes— but check with your accountant friend for the exact amount and how you should be paying it, if you're not sure. You also might find that leaving your earnings in a bank account or a PayPal account until a specific day of the week might make managing and tracking your money easier.

When people owe you money and they are not paying up, it's easy to get angry, which may stifle the creative process. Approach each collection call as though you are doing the client a favor. Be as pleasant and cordial as you usually are. If you are working for a small company or client, ask how much time they need to pay it in full. Most people will tell you they need 30 days. Send them a letter regarding your phone conversation and, more often than not, you will be paid because the time frame is the client's. If you have the stomach for this part of the process, which in the end can honestly drain you of most of your creativity, then congratulations, you've made the right career move! Check out these sites for further information in regard to setting fees: AllFreelanceWork.com and ConsultantJournal.com.

Yeah, I'm the Tax Man

It's not that scary to do your taxes as a freelance businessperson. Honest. But here's bit of advice. Just do them! Don't mess with the IRS. If you've earned more than $600 during the year on freelance projects, you are required to report that as self-employment income to the IRS. But here's the cool news. Just about anything you buy to perform your freelance work is a deduction, even your home office. Be sure to save your receipts as proof of your expenditures.

So grab a shoebox or if you feel like spending some of that hard-earned money, by a cool invoice holder at MyTaxBox.com and toss in those receipts. For help on what freelancers can deduct, check out

Wisebread.com, AllFreelance.com, and FreelanceSwitch.com. Some of the deductions that we usually claim are computers, printers, phone lines, certain books and magazines, paper, and some travel and dining.

All by Yourself

So now that we've given you some ideas and inspiration to set out on your own, we are setting you free. If you get lonely, join as many business networking groups as you can find to form alliances and get referrals. Sometimes you need a reason to shower and change out of your sweatpants and T-shirt. Keep an open mind, stay flexible and optimistic, and you'll escape the nine-to-five job rut forever. You now have the tools to make it on your own. You don't need us. Really. Get out of here. Shoo!

Treading Water in Creative Industries:

THE ART OF SELLING ART

"Look, it's my misery that I have to paint this kind of painting, it's your misery that you have to love it, and the price of the misery is thirteen hundred and fifty dollars."

—Mark Rothko

You've had creative urges all your life. You're an aspiring musician, composer, writer, artist, dancer, actor, comedian, or filmmaker. And you were fired from your damn day job—*again*! Only this time being downsized in a bad economy makes you look normal. Now you seem like an everyday working Joe who got caught in the latest wave of job cuts. For once, you're not the guy or gal with the "creative problem" your family worries about. Finally you're just like everyone else in America. But who wants to be like everybody else, right?

Assuming you have talent, check out the creative arts industry. You might just be the next John Grisham.

The term "creative industries" describes businesses with creativity at their core. Examples of creative industries are visual arts, crafts, music, literature, publishing, design, film and video, fashion, TV and radio, advertising, computer games, and the performing arts. When humans are worried, depressed, and frustrated, escape feels all warm and fuzzy. Art is a beautiful escape. When the going gets tough, a movie, song, great novel, or a funny joke is sought after. For example, Charlie Chaplin's comedy films became wildly famous in the 1920s, especially because he appealed to struggling immigrants and those going through tough economic times. Audiences loved Chaplin's character, the Little Tramp, the homeless, broke guy who used silly antics while he panhandled and struggled through life. The silent movies that Chaplin wrote, directed, and starred in made history as some of the greatest films of all time.

Cheap thrills are in demand, and if you're creative, now is the time to translate art into cash. Whether you compose music, literary works, visual art, or fashion, think about marketing and selling people a diversion—an experience of escape. The "art experience" is when art captures a person's attention and takes his mind away from its current state. Now that your day job is gone, think about how to earn money expressing yourself and providing a healthy diversion for people.

How Do I Use My Art to Earn Money?

You'll need to market and sell your talents. Business and art don't always naturally radiate from the same mind. The business and selling side of art often sucks when you hate it. But somebody has to do it—and that somebody doesn't have to be you. If business is not your passion and you're constantly aware that's it's a job, you'll do it half-heartedly. Consider teaming up with a business partner who will drive the selling end of whatever you create. Take advantage of all the unemployed sales and marketing people out there. Align yourself with someone who loves what you create and sees dollar signs in his eyes. Sharing your profit with someone who helps sell your art is better than making no money at all or earning money and loathing every second of it. You can use the tools in this chapter and our resource list to sell your own work or assign the task to a partner.

Make It Affordable

Discount stores rule in a down economy. Their evil plot to rule the world is to sell stuff to tons of people for a cheap and affordable price. This should be your blueprint for success. Thinking outside the box when you're in a cubicle isn't fun. Now that you're out of the box let the brainstorming begin!

Kitty Martini, co-author of this book, was an advertising copywriter by day and a stand-up comic at night. She's a single mom of two teenagers and relied on her copywriting job to pay the mortgage and support her family. She was fired from the day job, and her earnings from comedy gigs weren't going to cut it. With creative thinking, some business savvy, and a set of steel—uh—nerves, Kitty found a way to make a decent paycheck by telling jokes. Here's her story:

"I noticed that while the economy was tanking, fewer people were going to comedy clubs. The average comedy show at a club costs about $30 or $40, because there's an admission charge, a two-drink minimum, tax, and a tip. I also saw theaters, concert halls, and entertainment venues that required people to spend more than $20 were half empty a lot of the time. But movie theaters were packed on cheap movie night.

> *"Not only was I earning money, but I was creating jobs for other people and providing a way for audiences to vent."*

"Using cheap movie night as a business model, I decided to produce my own comedy shows in theaters with 200 to 300 seats—way more than the average comedy club. Would people come to see stand-up comedians perform if admission was only $10 and they didn't have to spend money on drinks? The first show sold out in three weeks. I called a few more theaters in other cities and started selling out more venues. Not only was I earning money, but I was creating jobs for other people *and* providing a way for audiences to vent.

"People really need to vent. So I decided to do something crazy. I hired an actor to play the role of a boss. I gave everyone in the audience a handful of marshmallows as they walked into the theater and let them throw them at the boss every time he walked on stage in between comedy acts. At the height of the show the entire theater looked like there was a snowstorm going on. TV stations and news reporters were calling, asking, 'What's this about people throwing marshmallows?' People who were as old as senior citizens and as young as college students were all behaving like third graders in a cafeteria food fight. Comedy had never been more fun. I was successful at making people laugh like little kids, and they in turn got to throw things and feel better—if only for an hour."

Can you think of a way to sell a product of your imagination for $10 or $20? Use what you learned in this book about Internet and viral marketing to get your art out there and a buzz going. If you're selling your art on T-shirts, prints, downloads of your music, or merchandise, be sure to market your craft to other parts of the world where currency is stronger than the American dollar. People will feel like they're getting an even bigger bargain if they can get the most for their money. Register for Yahoo! accounts in other countries. Post videos, if you can. Most social networking on sites such as YouTube, Video Yahoo!, and Metacafe are used by people around the world.

Become Famous on the Internet!

Darlene, a fired retail store manager, used online stores and social networking to launch her handmade greeting card business. She started selling greeting cards she designed and hand-printed at BigCartel.com, a free store where creative people can sell art, jewelry, handmade clothes, crafts, original music, and more. "I bought an old letter press printer from the 1800s and made old-fashioned-looking stationery, wedding invitations, and baby announcements," she said. "I never expected my little enterprise to be anything more than a way to learn the lost art of letter press printing. But business got exciting. I stared getting custom orders from huge nonprofit organizations and celebrities! Andy Warhol said everyone wants 15 minutes of fame. I haven't moved to Hollywood yet, but I got my 15 minutes!"

As far as we're concerned, Big Cartel is the best place to start if you can't afford to invest a lot of time or money in your artistic endeavor. It's also a good way to go if you only want to sell a few products (up to 100) and can't justify the expense of paying a Web designer to customize and maintain an Internet storefront for you. Monthly fees range from $0 to $19.99, depending on the number of products you're offering. There's no set-up fee, because Big Cartel has made it easy for the average computer user to design the site, upload the images, insert product information, receive payments, and maintain and update the Web pages. The only prerequisite is a PayPal premier or business account, which is necessary for receiving payments for product. As far as your artistic production line goes, you can start small with just a couple of products. In fact, if the number of products you're offering is less than five, using Big Cartel is free. If you want to offer up to 25 products online, it'll cost you $9.99 a month. For $19.99 a month, you can offer up to 100 products, but that's it. Big Cartel isn't for mass production. So give it a try; it's a little more artistic sounding than a garage sale!

Online art galleries that offer sales and reproduction services make it easy for you to market your fine art as framed prints, cards, posters, and calendars. When selling through online galleries, in most cases you set the price you want for your work, and the gallery adds its markup, takes orders, collects payment, and ships your work to the customer. The gallery sends you a check every month or when your profit goes over $50. It's a "turnkey" setup (which means there is a system already in place that will make it very easy to get started). All marketing materials and ad copy may be available. All these items greatly reduce the time for setup, thus making it a turnkey solution for you. Online art galleries such as RedBubble.com, ArtistRising.com, ImageKind.com, and ArtFair365.com, offer convenient services. They pay 15 percent or more commission on each item sold. Several free sites are available where you can run your own online art gallery. Another great place to start your artist storefront is through Etsy (Etsy.com)—"The place to Buy & Sell all things handmade." Etsy provides customizable storefronts to use as an online art shop for all types of artists and crafters, including fine art, photography, and fashion. They also offer payment collection through PayPal. Most important to an artist, Etsy members experience support and inspiration from fellow artists.

Check the resource guide at the back of the book for more listings. You also have the option of creating your own gallery and adding a shopping cart, but you'll have to find a company that reproduces and ships your work on demand. This arrangement is useful because you don't have to lay out any money for inventory that you might get stuck with if it doesn't sell out. To market your art, check out sites such as RedBubble .com, ArtCrush.com, and, of course, eBay.

Are you a musician? You can freelance in your field. You don't need a contract from a huge record company to sell your original songs.

Matt, a musician from Boston, tells us that being laid off was hugely beneficial to him: "I've been playing piano since I was five and earned my bachelor's [degree] in music. While trying to make it big in Nashville, I worked behind the front desk of a mortgage company. As the official 'lowest man on the totem pole,' I was essentially the canary in the coal mine when the mortgage business started to falter.

> "After four years of phone monkey by day, rock star by night, they brought me into the main office and informed me that my two-job lifestyle was about to become a one-job lifestyle."

"After four years of phone monkey by day, rock star by night, they brought me into the main office and informed me that my two-job lifestyle was about to become a one-job lifestyle. I think they were a little surprised when I didn't cry.

"This company was awesome enough to offer me a severance package that carried me for three months. I used that time to book a tour, find freelance clients who needed audio production or music, and otherwise ensure that I wouldn't *need* a new day job.

"It's been two years now and, though a lot of my friends and contacts are starting to face the same situation, I am still writing my own paychecks every month. Getting laid off was the best thing that ever happened to me!"

Matt sells his music online at Matthewebel.com and on CD. His music, which includes the song "Goodbye Planet Earth," is selling briskly and has received excellent reviews.

The Internet is an excellent place to sell your work, but remember to cover your assets! As an artist, you're in the idea business. First, you have to call yourself a creative entrepreneur. Then you need to turn your work into an "intellectual property." That's right; your work is your property. Get a patent or copyright that will protect your idea from commercial predators—those people who use your work to make money but don't bother paying you for it. Sites such as Copyright.gov and ProtectRite .com have the legal forms you need to file your intellectual property.

Once your work is protected, you can sell it directly and license your ideas. Licensing is renting or selling someone the right to capitalize on your intellectual property.

Virtual Marketplace, Real Money

There are several places you can network, sell, and cross-promote online. SecondLife.com, produced by Linden Labs in San Francisco, is a very popular and hip spot for all kinds of artists to promote their creations. It's a virtual world complete with its own store. Second Life avatars purchase goods and services with a currency called Linden Dollars, or L$. They sometimes pay to attend concerts and often tip the performers in the virtual venues. Others buy clothing and hairdos for their online personas. Linden Dollars can be converted into most of the world's currencies in the same way a foreign traveler might change dollars to euros. The going rate is about L$260 for US$1, according to the Second Life Web site. Artists sell their work online and in real life to online galleries, individuals, and companies. Several notable musical acts, including Suzanne Vega and Duran Duran, have already purchased "islands" (land) within the Second Life world where, as avatars, they can stream their live music concerts to their fans in real time. Playing a show in Second Life is done by sending a live music stream from the artist's computer to a Shoutcast server, and mapping the server's stream URL to a parcel of land in Second Life. People who visit the parcel in Second Life will immediately hear the live music stream. Musicians are also typically logged into Second Life during performance times, so they can chat with the audience between songs and even take requests.

Just because we suggest you sell your art in virtual worlds doesn't mean the Art Fairy will instantly zap you to Boardwalk—she won't. You need a marketing strategy. If you don't have a clue about how to strategize, get a few pointers from the experts who work with creative people. David Parrish, author of the book *T-Shirts and Suits*, helps creative people use cool business ideas. Parrish, who loves artistic types, advises large and small ventures worldwide and specializes in giving business advice to people like you. His blog, DavidParrish.com, discusses marketing, intellectual property, and business growth and development for creative people.

T-Shirts and Suits, which stands for "creativity and business," is also an international group for creative people in business within Facebook. To connect with people and find resources on Facebook, enter in the search box "advice for creative entrepreneurs."

"I try to build as many streams of income from my drawings as possible."

Phil designs digital robots for a video game. He owns the copyright for his designs and gets a cut of merchandise sales as part of his licensing agreement. "I try to build as many streams of income from my drawings as possible," Phil says. "The video game industry is constantly licensing the fantasy characters I draw. The industry seems to be exploding. I'm guessing that more and more people have time to play video games."

Does it pay to be a dreamer? The TED conference (Technology, Engineering, and Design), where the world's best and brightest talk about their ideas, touts this announcement on its Web site, TED.com: "Dream big. Because the world of ideas has never mattered more." We agree completely.

CHAPTER FOURTEEN

Filling the Money Pipeline:

INTERNET MARKETING OPTIONS

"Don't stay in bed, unless you can make money in bed."

—George Burns

Are you a people person who needs to work with a team? Or are you an antipeople person who prefers working in the company of pets? Some people prefer virtual fish and fake plants and nothing around that has to be spoken to or kept alive. Whatever you prefer, today's technology makes it easy for anyone to start an Internet-based business and use Internet marketing techniques to drive customers to a Web site and generate revenue. Yes, doing so is profitable—and we're not talking chump change here. If you have a great idea and can carry it out effectively, it's possible that Internet marketing can make you wealthy beyond belief.

Thirty-year-old Canadian, Markus Frind created an online dating company sitting in his apartment in Vancouver, British Columbia, with no business plan and no money. He called it Plenty of Fish. Frind owns the site and ran it himself from a desk in his bedroom with no employees. Frind capitalized on the fact that there are plenty of lonely people out there trying to hook up, but all the other dating sites charge a fee. Frind created a site that's free to anyone in the world who is looking for someone to date. His earnings come strictly from advertising revenue rather than membership fees charged to the users. According to *Inc.* magazine, in five years, it became the largest dating company in the English-speaking world and generates $10 million per year.

Ten mil? How can such a small company generate such huge profits? With the advertising and revenue programs that we'll tell you about, you'll be happy to know that you don't have to own a big company to profit like one.

Plenty of Fish is an unpresumptuous-looking Web site—crammed with rows of grainy, distorted thumbnail photos and personal ads—and it gets four times the traffic of the popular pay site Match.com. You make big money with an average-looking Web site if you're giving out something for free and it's good. Plenty of Fish has over a million users per day. Out of the $10 million in advertising revenue Frind collects, he pays himself a salary of $5 million per year. If you believe that Internet marketing is the same as the regular working world, you might think you'll have to work 90 hours a week for those millions. Nope. If you create a Web site that runs on its own, you'll hardly work at all. Frind claims to work one hour per day. "The site pretty much runs itself," Frind told *Inc.* magazine in an interview. "Most of the time I just sit on my ass and watch it." He spends the rest of his day playing video games, and hanging out.

Frind successfully beat his competitors (who have huge staffs, offices, and overhead) by offering the same service to the same market for free. The result? Approximately 1.6 billion ads posted, which brings in huge revenue checks from advertisers who want their ads viewed on each of those 1.6 billion Web pages.

A nine-to-five job may never serve you again after you've mastered a few ways to earn money with an Internet-based business. Here's an overview of some basic approaches to generating revenue via the Internet:

- Selling products or services
- Earning revenue from advertising
- Affiliate marketing
- Subscription or "pay-per-membership" Web site

What Kind of Web Site Can Earn You Money?

Any kind of Web site can earn big bucks. You don't have to sell stuff or even offer a service. Types of Web sites that earn revenue in different ways are online stores, blogs, sites that list information, classified ads, or services that people can subscribe to by paying a monthly fee. You can even earn revenue from social networking sites such as Facebook and Twitter.

With a load as light as your laptop and a few clever marketing tools you can peddle your wares to almost everybody on the planet. As soon as your Web site starts generating an income, you can burn your monkey suit and spend the rest of your career working in jeans, shorts, long johns, or a towel! Corporate headquarters might be the kitchen table, a coffee shop, or your bed.

It may take a little time for the payments to start rolling in, but not nearly as much time as it would take to start a traditional, off-line business.

These days, image is important, but personal branding is critical. It's not how slick you look, but how you relate to your customer base and what you are expressing to them. What kind of people do you want to reach? What look and "feel" will convey your service? Markus Frind took an honest, small-business-guy approach with Plenty of Fish. When you visit his site, you might stumble upon a personal announcement posted by Frind, like this one:

"Hello there and welcome! My name is Markus and I created Plenty OfFish.com because I was tired of seeing faceless corporations prey on people looking for love. Unlike paid dating sites, which have 500 to 800 employees whose jobs are to figure out how to get more of your money, this site is run by me, myself, and I. There are no employees. This site is my pet project and runs far differently than a paid site."

Business has gone full circle, from the small "mom-and-pop" store, to the giant corporation, and back to small business in the form of an individually run e-commerce site that can earn as much as a huge corporation. Except now it's not mom and pop—it's some chick or dude. You don't have to get a fancy college degree or even be an adult to make some serious bucks.

Ashley Qualls, a 17-year-old entrepreneur from Detroit, dropped out of high school and founded WhateverLife.com, which offers free MySpace layouts to young people who want to customize the look of their MySpace page. She began Web site design as a hobby at the age of nine, and eventually she created the site as a way to show off her designs. She started posting new layouts on her site, and her classmates started asking her if she could design custom layouts for their sites. She created dozens of new designs every week, and soon lots of kids were downloading them. Unable to afford the monthly price of Web hosting, she bartered her designs and got a Web host. WhateverLife.com exploded in 2005 when her Web host recommended that she sign up for an advertising program featured by Google called AdSense, a service that supplies ads to a site and shares the revenue.

Google AdSense is the simplest way to start monetizing a Web site. The program pays commissions generated from ads for other sites that appear on your Web site pages. For example, if you own a Web site and you sign up for Google AdSense, they pay you a small amount of money each time someone views the ad posted on your site. The dollars ad up quickly. The more people who visit the site, the more money is earned. Those little Web site ads that trim the outer edges of nearly every Web page you browse can rake in big bucks. How do these ads work? Usually, they're relevant ads that match your site's content and audience. For example, if you sell lawn fertilizer, Google will match your site with ads that appeal to people into gardening and beautifying their homes.

Depending on the type of ad people are viewing on your site, you can earn money from clicks or impressions. In Web advertising, the term "impression" is a synonym for "view," as in "ad view." AdSense pays you for the number of times an ad is seen (impressions) by someone who is viewing your Web site, and also pays you for each time someone actually clicks on one of those ads. If millions of people are looking at your site, then they're also viewing those AdSense ads. Because a single Web page can contain multiple ads, and a Web site contains multiple pages, we're not talking chump change here. Do the math. If 1,000 people look at your site, and there's 5 AdSense listings on each page, and your Web site is 10 pages deep, that's 5,000 views you'll be paid for each page the user looks at—plus even more money if your viewers click on those ads. Every month, Google sends you a check for the total amount of money the ads pay each time someone sees or clicks on them.

Ashley Qualls' first advertising revenue check from Google AdSense was $2,790, according to a report in *Fast Company* magazine. As her site gained in popularity, Qualls began earning as much as $70,000 per month generated by the millions of visitors to her Web site.

Qualls, Frind, and other madly successful Internet marketers follow a simple philosophy: target a niche market and fulfill their need with something that's free and attracts large numbers of people, then collect revenue from advertising programs. Companies other than Google AdSense that offer advertising revenue programs are ValueClick and VideoEgg.

More About Internet Advertising Programs

Exactly how much money do you get paid each time someone sees an ad on your Web site? You receive a portion of what the advertiser pays, and how much you earn depends on a number of factors, including how much an advertiser bids to pay for the ad and how many times the ad is viewed or clicked on. Google says the best way to find out how much you'll earn is to sign up and start showing ads on your Web pages. Every payment you get will give you an idea of how much traffic you're getting on your site and how many more people you need to attract to increase your revenue. The portion of money you receive per ad depends on how the ads are distributed. Google finds out what the advertiser wants to spend, then determines how frequently these ads will be posted. For example, if an advertiser only wants to spend $150 per month, its ad might show up on a few dozen Web sites. If a huge company such as Priceline or Hotwire wants to be seen on thousands of Web pages, it might pay Google millions of dollars to post its ads.

Page or ad impressions are tracked and recorded in a log that's maintained by the site server. In the case of Google AdSense, the more people you can attract to your Web site, the more ad impressions and clicks will be recorded, and the greater your revenue will be. If you're looking to earn revenue exclusively from AdSense, your best bet is to offer something free that will attract the most views as possible. If you ever wondered how sites that offer free listings, services, and information earn revenue, AdSense is one of the ways. Some Web sites are nothing but a list of ads for other Web sites! What's really cool is that AdSense is only one of several streams of income your Web site can crank, and it doesn't cost anything to set up.

How do you know how many clicks and impressions you're getting on AdSense? You can look at analytics. These are programs that monitor the activity on your site. Programs like Web Trends read the log, abstract meaning from it, and generate a report about site usage. Other programs, such as Central Ad, can keep track of all ad impressions that have been sent and how many of these were clicked on by users.

Where's My Money?

Google uses an Electronic Fund Transfer (EFT) payment system available in a number of countries. In order to get paid, your business has to have a bank account, and you have to be living somewhere in the world where there's a bank. AdSense earnings are delivered directly to your bank account every month without any additional effort. This seems really easy. If you think this is too good to be true, it's not! When we set up our blog, Jobs4YourFiredAss.com, it took us 20 minutes to tour the site and sign up for the program. After a few months we started receiving small payments from Google AdSense. The revenue motivated us to find more ways to increase visibility and visitors to our blog. If you find the instructions on Google AdSense too technical, visit eHow.com and in the search box, enter "how to use Google AdSense" to get a list of nontechnical instructions.

A Quick and Cheap Way to Start an Online Business

The basic way to start your venture is by first setting up a Web site. You don't have to buy products to resell or carry any inventory. You can set up a Web site based on your hobby or your expertise. The more specific your niche is, the bigger your profit will be. If you don't have the money to get a Web site designed, you can get a free site from Ning.com, Webs.com, BuildFree.org, or many others listed in our resource section. If you're selling items and you need to set up an online store, then Homestead .com or Big Cartel are a few options. They offer free design templates, shopping cart and pay tools, and even ways to add video!

You can chose the free Web site that best suits whatever you'll be selling. If you're reporting, touting your opinions and reviews, offering recipes, or pushing advice (like we are at Jobs4YourFiredAss.com), a free blog from Blogspot or Wordpress will do just fine. For blog ideas, check out the top moneymaking blogs listed in *Business Week*: Boingboing.com, ShoeMoney.com, ProBlogger.com, and PerezHilton.com.

Before Perez Hilton became the most famous gossip blogger, he was Mario Lavandeira. Lavandeira started out writing his Perez Hilton blog where he hung out—at The Coffee Bean & Tea Leaf in West Hollywood, California. Loaded with revenue-producing ads, merchandise for sale, and up-to-the-minute celebrity dirt, the blog is now one of the top gossip Web sites. Hilton calls it Hollywood's most hated Web site, but the advertisers love it!

Monetize = Generate Advertising Revenue = Cause Money to Land in Your Bank Account

Hilton, like other famous bloggers, started by writing content, then monetized his site. Anyone can set up a blog for free and receive weekly checks made up of advertising revenue by enrolling in ad programs such as Google AdSense. Then you work on attracting more and more people to visit your site by using SEO (search engine optimization), social networking, and viral marketing. Once you've caused zillions of people to look at and dig through your Web site, you can get out of hock and become a millionaire. Hopefully, you'll do something to help others and make the world a better place, like the people who developed all these cool free Internet marketing tools did.

If this news excites you, start dreaming up a Web site! We'll give you more ideas and tools you can use, and in our resource section you'll find more building blocks for your Internet marketing venture. It doesn't take a huge amount of money to get started, but it does take time and effort. Now is the perfect time to launch your Internet empire. With a profitable Web site, you may never have to depend on a job again.

When it comes to Internet marketing, any entrepreneur has a great shot at success, regardless of funding, location, size, or experience. The World Wide Web has massive potential.

AdSense isn't the only program you can use. As your traffic increases you can try CPM ads (cost per mille), which are ad campaigns based on a fixed number of impressions. Cost is quoted on 1,000 impressions. Other revenue-producing programs include CasaleMedia.com and ValueClick .com, and Nabbr.com, a revenue-sharing video widget.

Selling ads directly is another great profit maker. These are small boxes, ranging in size from a square inch or more, that display a business.

The ad can be viewed and also serve as a link to redirect the visitor to the advertiser's Web site. TechCrunch.com, a blog that reports Internet products and companies, earns $10 per month from advertisers who display on its home page. Once you've harvested a substantial number of page views, you can use this clout to pitch ad space. But more often, if you have huge traffic, companies will find you and offer you money so they can advertise on your site. *Inc.* reported that Markus Frind received a check for $180,000 from VideoEgg.com, a San Francisco company that paid him to run a series of commercials for Budweiser on Plenty of Fish. He'd never heard of VideoEgg until they contacted him. You can pitch ad space to businesses that share the same demographic as your site. Be sure to set up a simple Advertise page on your site to accommodate potential advertisers.

How to Earn Money from Affiliate Programs

You can be an affiliate of nearly any retail store or business out there. An affiliate is an existing business that pays you a commission for everything it sells to someone who goes through your Web site to reach theirs. You can set up a page that contains links to your affiliates and then market your affiliate's products with your Web site. For example, if you have an online travel agency, a company that sells types of luggage can be an excellent affiliate. Each time someone sees the company's ad on your site, clicks on it, and then buys some luggage, you earn a percentage of commission on the sale. Affiliate marketing is one of the fastest-growing and most lucrative Internet business models in the world. It allows anyone the opportunity to make money online by promoting various products or programs.

Unlike the situation when someone starts a traditional business, with affiliate marketing there is very little overhead and minimal barriers to getting started. Affiliate marketing can be a full-time career or a way to make part-time income. Launching your affiliate business is not as hard as you might think. There are thousands of affiliate programs throughout the Internet that cover a variety of different niches. Retailers can range from online stores to large department chains such as Wal-Mart and Macy's. Visit Linkshare.com to browse the assortment. Likewise, there are countless ways to promote these programs.

Here's an example: Vanessa was a burned-out Certified Public Accountant (CPA) from Atlanta who created a humorous, whimsical Web site that sold exotic-looking mismatched socks and trendy accessories for young, hip people with kids. "I was relieved when I got the pink slip," said Vanessa. "I didn't care if I had to live in a tent while I worked my Web site. After eight years of being bored and responsible, I wanted to play like a kid and be responsible. I got the idea when I realized I was tired of collecting every sock that the dryer ate and never finding its mate. I ordered colorful socks from crafters and wholesalers and made new "mismatched" pairs out of them. After learning how to earn income from affiliate marketing, I set up affiliate tabs on my sock site where people can click on links to retailers that sell other fun accessories like handbags and novelty clothes for kids, toys, and trendy accessories. Now I spend the day finding hip, young parents and sending links to my site. I don't earn as much as I did as a CPA, but every year my income grows and I'm getting orders from all over the world."

> *"Now I spend the day finding hip, young parents and sending links to my site. I don't earn as much as I did as a CPA, but every year my income grows and I'm getting orders from all over the world."*

You can create a Web site or blog solely dedicated to your affiliates or simply include affiliate links and banners on your existing Web sites. You can leverage existing traffic from your Web site or use PayPerClick advertising to send targeted visitors to any specific Web page. The goal is to get as many interested individuals to click through your affiliate links as possible. If you're an expert on a certain area of life, anything you recommend or talk about on your blog can include a link to an affiliate. Here's how it works: Let's say you have a blog that reviews TV shows, and you mention a show that's exclusively on DISH Network. If DISH Network is one of your affiliates, and your reader clicks on the link and then orders its service, DISH Network then pays you for the referral. The last time we checked, DISH Network pay $145 per referral, but the amount can vary, depending on which program you sign up with.

Helpful programs that will hook you up with affiliates in addition to Linkshare (Linkshare.com) are NetPartner (NetPartner.com), Revenue Allies (RevenueAllies.com), Affiliate (AffiliateMoneyMakingReviewSite .com), and Associate Programs (AssociatePrograms.com).

How to Create Income Using Premium Services

A premium service operates like a magazine subscription or HBO. Anyone who wants to use your Web site has to pay a monthly fee. Dating sites such as Match and Chemistry are popular examples of subscription Web sites. If you offer a service that provides such a valuable benefit to people that they would pay a monthly or yearly fee, the money is in members. If 5,000 subscribers pay $10 per month, then you're generating $50,000 a month. Not too shabby! Some sites that offer help and templates to launch a premium Web site are Sub Hub (SubHub.com), Wild Apricot (WildApricot.com), and Membership Site Owner (MembershipSiteOwner.com).

Give 'em *You*!

Did your parents ignore you? Were you super unpopular and felt unwanted? An inferiority complex is an awesome neurosis you can channel into personal branding— that is, creating a specific look or logo out of your name and turning it into a well-known brand. People who have turned their given names into products include fashion designer Tommy Hilfiger and TV chef Emeril (Lagasse). If insignificance made you feel bad, now it's leverage when your name is on T-shirts and in everyone's cupboard. One way to generate even more revenue from your Web site without increasing traffic or reach is to leverage the exposure your Web site generates to build your personal brand. You could offer your expertise at conferences as a paid speaker on specific topics or hold workshops or classes. Pushing your personal brand gives you the ability to connect with adjacent industries that might require your services or skills. If you love the attention but you hate talking to people, offer your superior words of wisdom on CD, DVD, and e-books!

Addict Them to Your Web site

Create your own social network, or as they say in Internet lingo, build "sticky communities." A great way to do this is by setting up a number of different sites using open source programs where users can sign up, post their profiles, and interact with one another. You can also create niche sites on one domain that offers specific bait, such as a recipe, game, cool product, band, or directory where people can click on and jump to your other sites. You can then cross-market all your existing sites to each other in order to keep your visitors coming back. You can create a community that shares a specific interest using Ning or any of the top 40 free open source downloads available at VivaLogo.com. You can create a social network for any kind of community. Whether it's cooking, motorcycle riding, organic gardening, or body piecing, for every niche in life, there's a bunch of people out there who would like to mingle and schmooze about it. There are scads of blogs that you can use as your gurus for learning tricks of the trade. Check out DoshDosh.com, which offers case studies and tips how to build a profitable online business.

Search Engines Are Your Friends

Finally, there's the matter of figuring out how to get your Web site to rank high on a search engine so the site can be found easily. This is called SEO, which stands for "search engine optimization." It's the process of improving the volume and quality of traffic by way of search engines such as Google and Yahoo! SEO figures out how search engines work and what people search for. If you don't know any nerds, this would be the time to find some and become their pal. Nerds are cool, and you should buy them beer. They can help you figure out how to optimize your Web site. Visit Meetup.com to find some in your town. Read search engine blogs that give you gold nuggets. For starters you can check out Search Engine Journal (SearchEngineJournal.com), SEOBook (SEObook.com), and Rae Hoffman's SugarRae (SugarRae.com).

A Web site that grabs loads of traffic is worth more than real estate. Once you create one, you can sell it for a ridiculously exorbitant fee, or keep it and continue getting filthy rich. When you hit your first million, send us an e-mail with a link to your goldmine and CC a copy to your former employer just to let them know that you're doing okay.

CHAPTER FIFTEEN

Ride the Worldwide Wave:
GO GLOBAL

*"Americans who travel abroad for the first time are often
shocked to discover that, despite all the progress that has been
made in the last 30 years, many foreign people still speak in
foreign languages."*

—Dave Barry

Remember back when you had a job? Recall how you used to hate every-thing about the place from the claustrophobic cubicle to the smelly break room? Did you used to gaze out the window on company time and dream of running off to live and work in a foreign country? Did you forget about those dreams, or were you just kidding yourself? Because, if you're reading this book, chances are you are unemployed. (We're not trying to make you feel bad. Millions of others are in the same situation.) Maybe you're having a tough time figuring out "what now?" Maybe that's because your dream of working abroad got lost in the unemployment line or forgotten in your panic to make the Corvette payments. That's where we come in. We're anticareer experts who want to guide you to put your happiness before work. You *can* have it all. Maybe you won't have as many material things as in the past, but you could be spending weekends hiking the Alps or eating real Chinese food in Taiwan after you finish this chapter.

Gary, who owned 50 percent of a successful freight forwarding company, was restless. He reached an agreement with his business partners, and they bought him out. In the final few months before he sold his business, another entrepreneur in a logistics-related industry offered him a position that made him a shareholder. Gary thought he would finally be happy.

"When I started to work in the business, everything seemed to be going fine until I began investigating some of the financial protection numbers for our potential clients," he explained. "Two months into the job, my business partner had me 'fired' by one of his employees."

"Two months into the job, my business partner had me 'fired' by one of his employees."

Dejected, Gary went to lunch and read the newspaper classified ads to keep his mind off the cruel turn his life had taken. "I saw an ad for a position, similar to mine, working with a foreign company in the same neighborhood," he said. "I called them after lunch, went over to see them. I was hired that afternoon at a higher salary and was to start work bright and early the very next Monday morning." This new job was one of the steps that eventually moved Gary to live in Asia. "Business is good," he said. "Life is great, and getting 'fired' by a guy I believe to be not the most honest and straightforward of business associates is maybe the best thing to happen to me, ever."

You Say Potato, I Say Kartoffel

One of the benefits of working abroad is that everything is new and different: the food, the air, the language, and the clothing. Sure, we have bread here in the States—*yawn*—but in Paris, when you buy a baguette first thing in the morning, the crust crackles and the inside is moist and chewy. *Viva la difference!*

Many countries, including the United Kingdom, France, and the Netherlands, offer free healthcare (no insurance premiums, deductibles, HMOs, or PPOs), and others such as Canada offer free child care and a college education and also great health benefits.

In 2008, the National Association of Colleges and Employers reported that 41 percent of employers across the globe were finding it more difficult to fill jobs, specifically openings for sales representatives, skilled manual trade people, and technicians in the areas of production/operations, engineering, and maintenance, according to results of Manpower Inc.'s 2009 Talent Shortage Survey. Certain countries with low unemployment, including Australia, the United Kingdom, Japan, and New Zealand, are hungry for accountants, architects, teachers, and engineers. If you are skilled as a graphic artist, ski or snowboard instructor, skydiving instructor, nurse, IT, anything in the medical field, journalist, or fashion designer, you should also consider working overseas. You may not be able to live there forever—some countries will eventually kick you out—but then you could move on to another country. For information on jobs, recruitment, and work permits, check out EscapeArtist.com, TeleportMyJob.com, OverseasManpower.Trade2Gain.com, and of course, Craigslist has jobs posted from all over the world.

Leaving on a Jet Plane

During these challenging economic times in the United States, many Americans are looking for greener pastures, but where to go? The most imaginative solution would be to start a nation of one's own. Unfortunately, it's almost impossible these days to buy an inexpensive uninhabited island, plant one's homemade flag on that rock, and declare that land a sovereign nation, but you could try.

But before you sell or walk away from your home and life, make sure you have what it takes to work thousands of miles away from your friends and family. Ask yourself a few basic questions: Are you a laid-back traveler, or do you need the comforts of the Ritz-Carlton? Do you love to try interesting new foods, or are you a picky eater? If you can't go with the flow on a regular basis, you should probably stay home unless you're up for the challenge.

Many expatriate workers have lost contact with friends, and others simply have "forgotten" to return home to the States to their families. Loneliness and depression are part of the job description in the beginning, but adventure, exotic locations, new languages, and cultural friendships may override the negativity. First things first: check out some more resources such as TravelSignposts.com, WorkingIn-Australia.com, and BBTworldwide.com to find out how easy or difficult it will be for you to find a new job, career, or life.

Once you've figured out where you want to live, you'll need to contact that country's department of labor and industry as well as its immigration department. You'll want to gather forms, read about requirements, and learn what immunizations and documentation you must have before you will be allowed to work there. It may seem like a hassle just for a "job," but with tenacity and good ol' know-how, you'll figure it out.

Let Uncle Sam Help

Our own government can give you a hand in finding a new career overseas in the Foreign Service—Careers.state.gov—but there's a test. A really hard test. If such a challenge interests you, e-mail the State Department for a study guide and sign up for the examination.

The last step in the process of moving across the pond or the border is securing a work visa. Without a visa they might let you in for a vacation, you'll still be unemployed, but the food at the homeless shelter might be Thai or French.

If your adventure turns out to be gritty and soul searching, be sure to keep a journal of your thoughts. You might find that you are a gifted poet, playwright, or novelist. Remember, back home, there's nothing profound happening at the mall.

Apply for a Visa and Work Permit

Many countries will give you a work visa for up to one year, and it's renewable in most cases, based on a point system according to your age, skills, and education level. There are other factors that may affect your ability to get a work visa. If you are bankrupt or have a criminal record, in most cases your work visa will be denied. For more information, check out the Web site of your country-of-choice. You can also click on TransitionsAbroad.com or maybe ExploringAbroad .com—both have a plethora of information on most countries—to see what type of documentation and application materials need to be sent to the appropriate government agency. While you are waiting for your application to be processed it would be a good idea to contact the U.S. Citizen and Immigration Service at USCIS.gov to see if you need to complete any additional paperwork in the United States before you say *ciao, sayonara,* or *adios* America. Other sites to gather information about your big move include OverseasDigest.com and AnAmericanAbroad.com.

If you don't want to stray too far from home, Canada—"America's Hat"—might be a good alternative. But beware, the Canadians won't let you just stroll over the border because you *sort of* talk like them. They do have a few restrictions on who is allowed to work in the country. The first requirement is that you must be able to provide a service needed in Canada that the Canuck job pool cannot fill. For example, professionals, including doctors, nurses, and technology experts, are all in high demand right now in Canada. Writers, actors, and other professionals in the movie and entertainment industry also face fewer restrictions on what they have to do to be allowed to work in the country. In some cases, these professionals don't need to apply for a work visa at all. For information about what you need to do to gain a Canadian work visa, check out the official site of the Canadian government at Canada.gc.ca.

Open for Business—Abroad

It takes guts to start your own business in a challenged economy, but starting a business in a foreign country . . . are you nuts? Maybe not. Good ideas are good ideas, no matter what is happening on Wall Street. Maybe you have a fantastic idea, and you know you can do it cheaper and better in another country. Let's see if we can help.

Before you fly over with your new gadget, recipe, or idea in your backpack, you might want to make several visits to the area to get an idea if your concept will even work. It's essential that you research your customer base. Doing so will allow you to assess local competition and network with potential business contacts.

If you're flexible about the country you may eventually call home, investigate to find out where there is a shortage for your skills or a gap in the market for your particular product. The biggest deterrent for people thinking of starting a business abroad is the language barrier. This limitation can be overcome either by learning, before you leave, basic conversation skills in the language by listening to tapes or taking classes or by hiring a multilingual member of staff. *Capiche?*

Sometimes the red tape will seem insurmountable, but when you think of all the years spent day dreaming in that cubicle, it will be worth it.

Adrian Leeds, an American who made a successful move to Paris, explains her incredible story of going global:

"We had caught the bug . . . the Paris *maladie,* we so lovingly call it. It's the 'itch' you 'scratch' by coming back time and time again until one day you do something zany because you just have to move to Paris. My husband, eight-year-old child, and I moved to a furnished apartment half the size of our Los Angeles home for life in the 17th *arrondissement.* We took French, joined organizations, enrolled our daughter in a bilingual school, explored the city, and made lots of friends. A year passed, but it wasn't enough. Once you've lived through four seasons in the world's most beautiful and romantic city, you can't go back to anything else. So, we stayed. I had been working since age 20 and had run my own advertising and marketing firm. I decided to write a resume and set out for job interviews. It didn't take long to discover that no one wanted to hire me. I had no official working papers, was too experienced, was considered to be too old, didn't know enough French, and most important, was too culturally American.

> "Working for no pay showcased my abilities and introduced me to the American community in Paris."

"The year passed with no success, so I took a different approach by working from the 'inside out.' The first open door was an opportunity to take on volunteer positions at an Anglophone organization, Women's Institute for Continuing Education, as coordinator of their French-English Conversation Group, as public relations director, and chairman of the development of their first Web site.

"Working for no pay showcased my abilities and introduced me to the American community in Paris—the authors, publishers, and media types. Little did I know that the work I would do there would be the foundation for everything to come.

"A sudden turn of events led to a tumultuous divorce in that third year, leaving my daughter and me stranded with a pittance of savings. The decision to stay instead of return to California was made by the good fortune of two offers: a freelance marketing job from the Web developer we hired to build the organization's Web site and an available apartment for rent in Le Marais, owned by a colleague at the same organization.

"Over the next 11 years, I kept an eye out for any opportunity. With a Web developer as a partner, I wrote the 'Insider Paris Guide to Good Value Restaurants' and published it online—the first of its kind. Other authors wrote guides, and the business flourished.

"With another partner, I started the Parler Parlor French-English conversation group. Eleven years later, it's still meeting three times a week and has welcomed several thousand people of more than 50 nationalities.

"Meanwhile, I wrote articles, networked with the community, and began publishing a communiqué for *Parler Paris*. Today it's the primary marketing tool for the entire enterprise with more than 17,000 readers (published twice weekly).

"Through networking and perseverance, a publisher and marketer at International Living discovered the foundation I had built and recruited me to open a Paris office. It was at that time that many new opportunities arose.

"We created a series of Living and Investing in France conferences and a variety of other workshops, primarily about writing. As of 2009, we will have held more than 25 real estate conferences under that name and dozens of other workshops.

"Business prospered, but I decided to strike out on my own, taking with me all that I had originally brought to the table. Presently, the Adrian Leeds Group, LLC consists of nine Web sites, a staff of more than 10 independent workers located in Paris, France, Europe, the United States, and Canada, plus it operates French-based business via its French counterpart, Parler-FranceEURL.

"There are still many lifelong dreams to fulfill. Paris is sure to be the inspiration for them, and I am confident that, before long, those dreams will turn into reality, just as so many others did with hard work and the courage to take risks without the fear of failure."

"There are still many lifelong dreams to fulfill. Paris is sure to be the inspiration for them, and I am confident that, before long, those dreams will turn into reality, just as so many others did with hard work and the courage to take risks without the fear of failure."

Bon Voyage, Don't Forget to Write!

As you embrace the global lifestyle, meet new people, and make new friends, your life will possibly become an adventure, something you might never have experienced if you hadn't lost your stupid job in the first place.

When a comic is on stage and the red light goes on, it means his time is up. Before he leaves the stage, he says, "and I'll leave you with this. . . ." So, we will leave you with this: you can be happy and successful doing something you love. Hopefully the worst is over. Now you can enjoy being in the moment, and the challenges you have been facing will make you stronger and a better person. Your luck changed the day you picked up this copy of *Thank You for Firing Me!*, which will continue to guide you toward making intelligent career choices for years to come. So get on with your life. Go on . . . *get out of here*. We're not firing you, but we *are* letting you go.

Conclusion

> *"Choose a job you love and you will never have to work a day in your life."*
>
> —Confucius

Many books on finding a job or a new career are filled with tips on creating attention-grabbing resumes, honing your interview skills, and how to write that ideal thank-you note. These books are of course necessary in your hunt for the perfect employment opportunity and their importance on your bookshelf should not be dismissed. However, so many people are unemployed these days that they are desperate and will take any job that is offered, finding themselves back in the very same place they started—miserable, exhausted, and without hope. And that's exactly what we don't want for anyone. Not for *you* and not for *us*.

During the first big wave of layoffs, before anyone said the word *recession* out loud, we were downsized from our own jobs. Writer Kitty Martini's lucrative position at an ad agency vanished and freelance journalist Candice Reed received fewer and fewer assignments from newspapers. Kitty was fired, and Candice went from receiving 60 to 30 to 15 assignments per month . . . to none.

It wasn't long before we noticed that some of our friends were beginning to lose their jobs as well. Soon after that, the media blasted out the astonishing news that unemployment "soared" to a historical high of 6.7 percent—the highest since 1974. The year's total job losses were at 1.9 million. That's when we realized we weren't alone.

When we began hatching the idea for this book, Kitty was freshly fired, depressed, and eating M&M's for breakfast. Candice's last job interview at a public relations firm was with a human resource person who was wearing flip-flops and a visible belly ring. The interview didn't go well. Kitty would have gone for another copywriting job, but she realized she was burned-out and didn't want to write another ad again. She wanted to write jokes.

When we met to discuss the book we would complain about our own financial problems. But we would also laugh. We would whine about the difficulty in finding new jobs and moan about how hard it was to make ends meet. And we would laugh some more because really, what else could we do? We kept thinking, "What kind of work could two unemployed writers with about 50 years of experience between the two of us and who laugh at almost everything do in this new economy?"

To escape reality, our conversations kept going back to the things we'd always wanted to do: Kitty wanted to write jokes and do stand-up comedy full-time, and Candice wanted to finish writing her novel. We didn't want to go back to an office job out of desperation, and we convinced ourselves that we didn't have to. We became excited about our future again. We realized that being out of work was actually a *good* thing. Kitty didn't have to get up early in the morning, which meant she could perform at comedy clubs every night. Candice was relieved she didn't have to wear a belly ring to conform. She could work on that novel while looking for writing positions.

We knew we had to do more than just survive because being down-sized isn't easy. But we wouldn't give up. We found part-time gigs to pay the bills, made deals with our creditors, and cut back on everything. We didn't want to simply *survive* a financial crisis, we wanted to *succeed*. We also realized that we wanted to transform misfortune into opportunity and help others do the same. The excessive good times were over for everyone and we had to create our own jobs and somehow ride a new wave of success. And that's when the idea of *Thank You for Firing Me!* was born.

> *"We also realized that we wanted to transform misfortune into opportunity and help others do the same."*

The great thing about a crisis is that people start pulling together to seek support and help from each other. People are nicer and more willing to listen and help during tough times. In this climate of sharing resources and working together, we felt everyone could use a few laughs and some practical information on how we can all reinvent ourselves and be agents of change in a changing world.

While writing the book we heard from hundreds of people who chronicled their anecdotes of how they created a more fulfilling life after losing their jobs. People shared their personal stories of change and success over the phone, via e-mail, and at our live comedy show where we encouraged people to vent and laugh about work. These stories were proof to us that we could all reinvent ourselves.

You'll note that nowhere in this book did we ever say that finding a new career or job that you love would be easy or happen overnight. Some days you may find life really hard to endure when no one returns your calls or you can't land an interview. But keep at it. You're not alone. The economy has lost six million jobs since the recession began in December 2007, the most of any downturn in the post–World War II era, but there is a light at the end of the tunnel and we hope you found it in the pages of this book.

As you go from soul searching to job searching, we trust we will make you feel better about your situation. Whether you still live in your big, refinanced house (perhaps with loan modifications) or in a camper in the Wal-Mart parking lot, we hope you can laugh just a little at the situation. Each day think about what we've written and take to heart the inspiring stories that others have shared. We want to hear your story, and we look forward to you telling us about your progress. (Write to us at ThankYouForFiringMe.org.) Step-by-step you will inch closer to your dream job and a more fulfilling life. Before you know it, the economy will have turned around again and you'll be riding the next wave of success in the new economy and shouting, "Thank you for firing me!"

Resource Guide:

CATCHING THE NEXT WAVE OF SUCCESS
AFTER YOU LOSE YOUR JOB

There are many people in this world—*and you know who you are*—that buy books and immediately flip to the last page to see how it ends. We would hate to think that *you* didn't read the last few hundred pages of *Thank You for Firing Me!* but, if that's how you work then so be it. Listed here are more resources and Web sites for your job search that correspond with the chapters in this book. Use this convenient list if you're in a rush to launch your next career. When you land your new gig, be sure to drop us a line at ThankYouForFiringMe.org.

CHAPTER ONE: Reconnect Before You Rebound

We know you're freaked out, stressed out, and nervous as hell, but relax. Watch a reality show and see how great you actually have it. Then, when you stop shaking, peruse this list of resources pertaining to Chapter One. The Web sites listed will help you find a way to start making it in the job world again and if nothing else, get you to turn the computer back on.

Certified Career Coaches
Certified career coaches provide professional career coaching services. Find a career coach by searching this extensive database at no cost.
> CertifiedCareerCoaches.com

Brazen Careerist by Penelope Trunk—How to Find a Career Coach
Weaknesses are hard to beat, so if you're really serious about making a personal change, this expert recommends a career coach.
> PenelopeTrunk.com

Career Coach Institute—Career Coach Training, Career Coach (Career Coach Training Career, Coach Certification Career, Coach Classes, Career Coach Institute)
There's no better time to become a coach—so find out if it's right for you!
> CareerCoachInstitute.com

Coaching Tip—The Leadership Blog: Persuasion Power

Coach John G. Agno is your own cultural attaché; keeping you abreast about careers while teaching you to inspire.

CoachingTip.blogs.com

HowToDoThings.com—How to Keep Yourself Motivated

Often, when we get ourselves ready to do something, we are not happy to do it. No matter how hard we try, the task just seems difficult, boring, or both. If you search for "How to keep yourself motivated," you'll be rewarded!

HowToDoThings.com

Rockport Institute—Career Change Counseling, Career Coaching, and Aptitude Test Services

For a career change or how to turn your passion into a paycheck—career coaching to design the perfect career matching your talents, personality, passions.

RockportInstitute.com

Bialla—Executive Job Search

If you're an ex-big shot and you like what you do, check out this great executive search Web site.

Bialla.com

Helpguide—Preventing Job Burnout: Signs, Symptoms, Causes, and Coping Strategies

Job burnout: know the signs and symptoms. Find out if you're at risk of job or workplace burnout and what to do if you are.

HelpGuide.org

Career Planning on About.com—Signs of Job Burnout and Results

You may experience periods of burnout due to overwork, a difficult boss, or something else. Learn more about the symptoms and the results of burnout.

CareerPlanning.about.com

ADD [Information] on About.com—Jobs for Individuals with Attention Deficit Hyperactivity Disorder (ADHD)

Some adults with ADHD have compensated by structuring their day and are extremely organized.

ADD.about.com

whfhhc.com—Jobs for People with Attention Deficit Disorder (ADD) and High Anxiety and Depression Problems
whfhhc.com (keyword: depression)

CHAPTER TWO: Getting the Most Out of Drifting

Okay, you're still depressed and tired, and we don't fault you for that. But look around—everyone is walking around with a cloud over their head, so it's time for you to set an example. Go outside and get some vitamin D. Talk to your neighbors, and assure them you're still alive. Now come back in and be inspired by the books, blogs, and Web sites that are relevant to Chapter Two.

Web Sites to Peruse Other Than Gossip Sites

About Genealogy (Genealogy.about.com)—Planning a Perfect Family Reunion
This handy family reunion software program from FormalSoft is designed to help you organize your reunion and even create a family reunion Web site. We recommend that you gather your family around you for support in your search for a new life and job.
Genealogy.about.com

Family Reunion WebRing
Family Reunion WebRing is a selection of family, personal, and other Web sites that involve families that are having or have had a reunion.
WebRing.com

My Life
Find your high school classmates, old friends, friends, alumni, and class reunions at MyLife.com.
MyLife.com

Find a Friend—High School and Military College Class Reunions
Find a friend, high school or college alumni, or military school classmate from more than 40 million members in over 200,000 affiliations.
FindAFriend.com

Facebook

Facebook is a social utility that connects people with friends and others who work, study, and live around them. People use Facebook to keep up with friends and family.

Facebook.com

TeeBeeDee—Sharing Experience to Thrive

TeeBeeDee is the online information network for those over the age of 40. Find free information from members and experts about career change, work transition, and dating.

TBD.com

Genkvetch

Not to be outdone by the younger generation, Genkvetch helps seniors find friends and network with others on this site. The type on this site is in big font for those people who refuse to admit they need glasses. There are articles on health, news, and even volunteer opportunities.

Genkvetch.com

Breakthrough to Success—Blog to Help You Achieve Success

Lynn Pierce, the Success Architect, has taught people how to combine business and personal development to reach the pinnacle of success and live their lives.

YourBreakthroughToSuccess.com

Breakthrough to Success Home Study Course

This is Jack Canfield's Proprietary 7-Day Breakthrough to Success Workshop, which is purported to change lives, multiply incomes, increase time off, and dissolve stress.

StudyWithJack.com

Great Books to Read Now That You Have the Time!

Dan Baker, PhD, *What Happy People Know: How the New Science of Happiness Can Change Your Life for the Better*, Rodale Books (January 4, 2003)

Baker is a psychologist and director of the Life Enhancement Program at Canyon Ranch in Tucson, Arizona. In this book he shows you how to look at unhappiness in an entirely new way. He believes that people can learn to be happy instead of remaining trapped in a vicious cycle of stress. The exercises in his book work—we've tried them ourselves—and they show you how to disable the fear that is holding you back from finding that perfect job.

Jean-Louis Serven-Schreiber, *The Art of Time: Gain New Mastery over Your Life and the Power to Live Your Time Instead of Simply Spending It,* 2nd ed., Da Capo Press (August 31, 2000)
This succinct book is insightful and gets right to the heart of time and time management. You will want to read it many times over to master the art of multitasking—something you'll need to learn whether you land a job with a great company or you begin working for yourself.

Kathleen Norris, *Acedia & Me: A Marriage, Monks, and a Writer's Life,* Riverhead Hardcover (September 16, 2008)
This compelling memoir follows Norris as she slips into apathy after the death of her husband. But wait, it's not a downer because her stories are personal and inspiring to those of you sitting in your Lay-Z-Boy recliner crying about the way your life has spun out-of-control. This book is a much needed kick-in-the-ass for all the couch potatoes out there who haven't even started looking for a new life.

Neil Fiore, *Awaken Your Strongest Self: Break Free of Stress, Inner Conflict, and Self-Sabotage,* McGraw-Hill (September 8, 2006)
Yes, this is a self-help book, but face it, you need all the tools you can get in this confusing job market. This book will explain to you exactly what you are doing wrong and how you are sabotaging your life. Fiore teaches you how to set goals and get back out there and take charge of your life again.

CHAPTER THREE: How to Ride the Tides of a Changing Job Market

We're going to say that scary word again . . . are you ready? *Change!* It's an ugly word to many people, but in today's world you have to rethink your ideas about careers, money, and, well, just about *everything* has gone nuts. If you're not changing with it, you'll be left behind, it's as simple as that. Let's face your fears head on and see what types of sites we can find that can hold your hand and maybe give you a virtual hug as you become a part of this new economy.

AcademicInfo—Online Courses and Classes in Personal Development

Find accredited online personal development courses, classes, and training programs covering art, music, photography, personal finance, writing, and more.

AcademicInfo.net (keywords: online courses, personal development)

Landmark Education—Seminars, Courses, and Landmark Forum

Landmark Education offers the Landmark Forum, graduate courses, and seminars and is a global leader in training and development.

LandmarkEducation.com

WorldWideLearn—Personal Development Courses and Training for Self-Improvement

Personal development education online with courses, tutorials, classes, and tools to help you on your quest for self-growth.

WorldWideLearn.com (keywords: online courses, personal development)

Anthony Robbins Companies

Anthony Robbins has coached countless high-level business leaders and politicians, and now you can use the same strategies to reach the top.

TonyRobbins.com

Meetup

Meetup makes it easy for anyone to organize a local group or find one of the thousands already meeting up face to face.

Meetup.com

Procrastination Forum—Groups to Help Solve Procrastination

Here is a group where members support one another in overcoming procrastination.

ProcrastinationHelp.com

LifeOrganizers.com—How to Organize Your Home and Office, Organizing Tips

LifeOrganizers.com is a rich resource of office and home organizing articles, tips, and fresh, easy ideas on how to get rid of clutter from every part of your life.

LifeOrganizers.com

NetPsychology—Exploring the Online Delivery of Mental Health
NetPsychology explores the uses of the Internet to deliver psychological and healthcare services; its focus is exclusively on online resources.

Psychology.info

iWorkWithFools.com—Anonymous Sharing of Work-Related Stories
Welcome to iWorkWithFools, where you can read or anonymously share work-related stories about the foolish coworkers and bosses with whom we all deal daily.

iWorkWithFools.com

Passion Catalyst—Curt Rosengren
Curt is a passion catalyst, working with people to help them identify their passions and create a career.

PassionCatalyst.com

CHAPTER FOUR: How to Be Powerful:
Reeducation for Reinvention

If you feel the need for keggers and sorority girls or fraternity boys, going back to school to learn a new skill may be the best place for you. Whether you learn through an online course or you walk onto a campus, it's never too late to learn. Just stay away from the beer bongs, and for goodness sake, don't even think of streaking!

BartendingSchools.com—Directory of U.S. Bartending Schools
BartendingSchools.com

Coach Training Alliance—Life Coaching Certification
If you are the go-to person when friends are looking for answers, check out this site and earn your life coaching certification in just six months.

CoachTrainingAlliance.com

International Coach Federation (ICF)

ICF is a nonprofit, professional organization that represents personal and business coaches.

CoachFederation.org

Makeup Designory (MUD)

In addition to teaching you how to become a makeup artist and apply makeup for fashion and the movie industry, the school has its own cosmetics line, with makeup supply retailers in the United States, Japan, and Australia.

MUD.edu

Academy of Performing Arts in Clowning—First Internet Clown School

Learn clowning and clown school skills: clown makeup, balloons, magic, and more.

ClownSchool.net

National University (NU)—Accredited Online, On-Campus College Degrees

California's leader in adult education and accelerated learning offers online university courses, distance education, and continuing education programs.

NU.edu

Concord Law School—Online Law School, Online Law Degree

Obtain your law degree online from Concord Law School.

ConcordLawSchool.edu

American Truck Driving School Directory

Over 250 free and tuition CDL Class A truck driving schools for truck driver training across America.

Infoporium.com

Kelly Services—Temp Jobs

Kelly Services provides staffing services and employment opportunities globally.

KellyServices.com

CHAPTER FIVE: Staying Afloat: Finance Your New Life

Just because our country is broke doesn't mean you will be, too. Even though the national debt is somewhere around a gazillion dollars, we still like to think there's some moola stashed in the bottom of the cookie jar of life. Treasure hunts are fun, right? Stock up on the ramen noodles and start hunting for capital here.

My Own Business Inc.
> *The Internet's top free start-a-business course. Learn how to write a business plan, pick a business, sign a lease, tackle small business accounting, and much more.*
>> MyOwnBusiness.org

Credit Unions Online—List of Reliable Credit Unions
> *Credit Unions Online features a credit union directory by city and state.*
>> CreditUnionsOnline.com

CAMEO: California Association for Microenterprise Opportunity
> *CAMEO seeks to reduce the wealth gap in communities by promoting economic opportunity through microenterprise development.*
>> Microbiz.org

Small Business Administration (SBA)
> *The SBA offers numerous loan programs to assist small businesses. Note: the SBA is primarily a guarantor of loans made by the U.S. government.*
>> SBA.gov

National Venture Capital Association (NVCA)
> *This association aims to foster greater understanding of the importance of venture capital to the U.S. economy and to support entrepreneurial activity.*
>> NVCA.org

Abilities Fund
> *This fund helps disabled people learn how to start a small business. Also, it offers some financial support with start-up costs.*
>> AbilitiesFund.org

Rural Development, Business, and Cooperative Programs (RBEG)
The RBEG program provides grants for rural projects.

RurDev.USDA.gov

NAIC Online
The National Association of Investment Companies (NAIC) is the membership organization for firms dedicated to investment in the United States.

NAICvc.com

CHAPTER SIX: Your Support Network: Don't Bail Out!

What would a rock star be without roadies? What would a bowling league be with one guy holding a ball? And what would you be if you tried to make your career happen all by your lonesome? Answer: lame! Don't slow dance alone at a wedding. Don't talk to yourself out loud in a crowd. And don't make another career move without reaching out to your support networks for help.

Meetup
We've mentioned this site before, but just in case you're skipping around this section and haven't experienced this site's many types of groups, here it is again. You can start and organize your own meet-up group or join one in your neighborhood. Just enter your interests in their search box, and find out what groups match what you're looking for.

Meetup.com

Job-Hunt
This is a huge list of job hunting resources, and there's a whole bunch of networking groups you can find out about here.

Job-Hunt.org

LinkedIn
This site provides access to over 30 million professionals. Okay, you probably don't have time to meet all 30 million, but you can at least make some connections, exchange information, ideas, and opportunities. Stay informed about your contacts and industry. Find the people and knowledge you need to achieve your goals.

LinkedIn.com

Riley Guide

This site has a load of information about job hunting and listings on where you can find networking and support groups. Hit the Networking tab or enter "support" in the search box.

RileyGuide.com

VentureStreet

This is an online business listing network where you can join and interact with business owners, networking groups, and potential clients.

VentureStreet.com

Mastermind Groups

This site has a forum, blog, and tips on how to use a mastermind group to succeed. If you're new to the concept of a mastermind group then check out this book: Napoleon Hill, Think and Grow Rich, *Ballantine Books (May 12, 1987). You can download it for free in PDF format or purchase the print book from Amazon.*

MastermindGroups.org

The Success Alliance

Essentially, this site is a mastermind group for the self-employed. Members meet every other week for a 90-minute telephone group mastermind conference call, facilitated by a small business coach.

TheSuccessAlliance.com

Mastermind Forums

This site provides online business mastermind team tips.

Mastermind-Forums.com

Social Networking: Make Some Friends, Already!

Just in case you're not brave enough to start hustling yet, start by joining some social networks online. But please—don't use them as an excuse to stay in the house. Think of these sites as a way to start finding out who is doing what. Then put down the potato chips and get out there!

Friendster.com, Facebook.com, MySpace.com, Tribe.com, YahooGroups.com, Twitter.com

CHAPTER SEVEN: Your Winning Game Plan:
How to Achieve a Life You Love

Are you feeling brave enough to stop playing *Warcraft*, leave your virtual world domination games behind, and start putting together a real-life strategy? We don't want your plan to suck. You'll need a strategy that sets you apart from the masses and makes you stand out. Here's what we recommend!

Web Sites to Check Out

Blue Ocean Strategy
They tout that the aim is not to outperform the competition in the existing industry but to create new market space and make the competition irrelevant. BOS offers a set of methodologies and tools to create new market space. You can also order the book on their site.
> BlueOceanStrategy.com

CareerBuilder
Find some juicy tidbits, articles, advice, and job strategies for your game plan here.
> CareerBuilder.com

Jobacle
Find career advice, employment news, and job Web site reviews. The Jobacle blog and podcast delivers everything work-related with a healthy dose of reality.
> Jobacle.com

Brazen Careerist
Like a great hot dog, it's worth the repeating: this blog rocks! Though it's written by and for young people, it's a great way to get related to twenty-first-century strategy. Subscribe and find out the latest strategies shared by some of the most brilliant young minds in the working world.
> BrazenCareerist.com

mybusinessbooks.com
Don't get overwhelmed with all the books on this list, but you'll find a few golden nuggets here.
> mybusinessbooks.com

Jobs 4 Your Fired Ass
Subscribe to our witty, newsy blog, share your troubles, post comments, and be our pal. We'll do our best to dig up helpful information for your game plan.
Jobs4YourFiredAss.wordpress.com

Thank You for Firing Me!
At last, career help that's practical and funny! This is our official Web site, where you'll find entertaining, informative advice from anticareer experts Kitty Martini and Candice Reed. Here you can share your stories and videos, and find news about unique job and business opportunities. Come visit us. Laughter will empower and energize you!
ThankYouForFiringMe.org

Book on How to Figure Out a Killer Game Plan

Molly Fletcher, *Your Dream Job Game Plan: Five Tools for Becoming Your Own Career Agent*, Jist Works (November 3, 2008)
Fletcher gives real honest advice on how to find a real honest job! She knows what it takes since she was the top female sports agent in the country. That's right: show us the money!

CHAPTER EIGHT: Big Waves Ahead:
Hot Green Industries Coming Your Way!

Here's your chance to get out of the rat race and shift toward a green economy that will reduce carbon emissions and lift people out of poverty. Wow! Making money *and* earning karma points—could it get any better? Turn your white or blue collar a nice shade of green and jump feet first into this rapidly developing field. We found so many sites, but we couldn't list them all. Be sure to check additional listings at Jobs4YourFiredAss .wordpress.com and ThankYouForFiringMe.org. Just remember when you're rolling in it who gave you the idea in the first place.

SunEdison, Computer, Tech, and IT Jobs
Search and apply for SunEdison tech jobs, computer and IT jobs listings.
Tech-centric.net

SunEnergy Power Corporation Management

SunEnergy Power Corporation presently has the need for independent sales consultants in commercial solar power . . . plus many more personnel needs.

SunEnergyPower.com

Suniva—A World Leader in PV Technology Careers

Come join the hottest team in solar! Suniva is actively recruiting the best and brightest in the business.

Suniva.com

AVA Solar—Career Opportunities

AVA Solar has developed a thin-film photovoltaic (PV) module manufacturing technology that is the culmination of more than 15 years of scientific and engineering effort.

AVAsolar.com

Ausra—Jobs, Utility-Scale Solar Power

Are you interested in joining a company that will generate renewable electric power on a massive scale? Then Ausra is for you!

Ausra.com

Borrego Solar Systems—Solar Construction Project Manager

Borrego Solar's approach to compensating their employees is unique and they promote from within. Check them out because they are looking for career-minded employees.

BorregoSolar.com

Chesapeake Solar LLC—Solar Power Solutions

Chesapeake Solar, a "groSolar" company, is currently seeking qualified solar installers.

ChesapeakeSolar.net

eSolar—Utility-Scale Solar Power

They are currently recruiting engineers with solid experience and a passion for working on software, electrical, thermal, and mechanical projects for our solar plants.

eSolar.com

SolFocus

In North America some of the actual job listings in the past have included engineering and senior reliability engineer. If you feel like some takeout, try job listings for Asia, which have included senior optical supplier quality engineer and senior opto-mechanical supplier.

SolFocus.com

Careers at SunRun
If you're looking for a job in the solar industry, SunRun has lots of exciting career paths to offer.

SunRunHome.com

Solyndra
With the rapid growth in the solar energy industry, it's a great time to join Solyndra, a young and dynamic start-up based in Fremont, California.

Solyndra.com

Van Jones
Van Jones, *The Green Collar Economy: How One Solution Can Fix Our Two Biggest Problems*, HarperOne (October 7, 2008)
Don't forget to check out this expert's Web site for more green information.

VanJones.net

CHAPTER NINE: Working for Gen Y? Why Not!

Generation Y will one day rule the world, and you'll want to make sure you don't end up not knowing what the hell is going on. Do names such as Twitter and Digg sound foreign to you? Well omg, ru gtg? No? Then I m rofl! If you want to work for this generation, or if you are this generation, then you should find these sites helpful in finding a career or business aimed at getting some cash from approximately 70 million of these consumers.

Urban Dictionary
This is a searchable archive of contemporary American slang, listed in alphabetical order.

UrbanDictionary.com

Twitter: What Are You Doing?
Twitter is a free social messaging utility for staying connected in real time.

Twitter.com

YouTube—Broadcast Yourself
Share your videos with friends, family, and the world.

YouTube.com

Digg—All News, Videos, and Images
Digg is a place for people to discover and share content from anywhere on the Web.

Digg.com

popurls—The Original Buzz Aggregator
popurls is the mother of aggregators, a single page that encapsulates up-to-the-minute headlines from the most popular sites on the Internet.

popurls.com

Jobster—Viral Marketing Jobs
Visit Jobster and enter "viral marketing" in the keyword search box.

Jobster.com

Research 247—Market Research Jobs, Vacancies, and Careers
The site provides recruitment specialists solely for the market research industry. View market research jobs, vacancies, and careers online.

Research247.com

GreenBook JobSource—Find Market Research Jobs or Job Candidates
The GreenBook JobSource is an online career and job center connecting employers with qualified market research and marketing professionals.

GreenBook.org

7 Studios
7 Studios is the developer of games such as Legion: Legend of Excalibur *and* Defender. *Having produced games based on both film and television, this group is uniquely suited to work with film studios and producers who would like to see their properties become successful interactive games.*

SevenStudios.com

5TH Cell—Advancing Entertainment
5TH Cell is the creator of Drawn to Life *and* Lock's Quest. *The ideal job candidate has experience working in games or information*

technology, and is passionate about problem solving. Hit the Jobs tab.

5THCell.com

Gamasutra Independent Games Festival

Folks at Gamasutra are always on the lookout for great people to join their team in design, programming, animation, and 2D/3D art.

Gamasutra.com

Wikipedia.org—Game Industry

Find a comprehensive list of video game companies and their job sites. Enter "Video Game Industry" in the search box.

Wikipedia.org

CHAPTER TEN: Banking on Boomers

Baby boomers may still wear tie-dyed shirts and sandals, rock out to "Lite Hits" stations, and expound on the "glory days," but that's cool. There is money to be made from this youthful generation, whether you're 22 or 72. Find an area in this list that gets you excited, such as travel or health-care, and start your new career, making money from these Joni Mitchell–singing, macramé-loving ex-hippies. It's all groovy!

Travel Job Wire—Travel Industry Jobs

Looking for a great travel job or successful travel career? Search and apply online for open positions in the travel industry.

TravelJobWire.com

Airline Job Finder—Airline Jobs, Airport Jobs, Aviation Industry

Whether you're an experienced air travel industry worker or someone seeking to break into the industry, Airline Job Finder can provide the help you need.

AirlineJobFinder.com

Cruise Ship Jobs

New World cruise ship employment agency provides information on cruise ship jobs. Travel in style around the world aboard a luxury cruise ship for free while earning a paycheck.

CruiseShipJobs.com

Healthcare Jobs—Healthcare Jobs Career Center for Medical Jobs
The site lists many resources to find and explore healthcare jobs, medical jobs, hospital jobs, and home healthcare careers.

Healthcarejobs.org

Activity Director Jobs
Activity director jobs, therapeutic recreation, recreation therapy, activity therapy, creative arts therapy, and activity director jobs are posted here.

ActivityJobs.com

MedHunting—Medical and Healthcare Jobs
Search and post healthcare jobs and medical jobs on this free site.

MedHunting.com

HealthCareJobs.org—Home Healthcare Jobs, Career Exploration, and Job Resources
Home healthcare jobs and careers with related resources are provided here. Enter "home care" in the search box.

HealthCareJobs.org

HealthCareerWeb—Medical Jobs and Healthcare Job Search
Find nursing jobs and healthcare jobs within hospitals and medical offices nationwide. In addition, join MedCom to connect to healthcare professionals.

HealthCareerWeb.com

BOOMERNET—Jobs for Boomers
This is the job search site focused on connecting experienced and retired workers with potential employers.

BOOMERNET.com

Baby Boomer Magazine Online—Complete Resource for Baby Boomers
Baby Boomer *magazine is a complete resource magazine for the baby boomer generation including health, diet, fitness, exercise, travel, vacations, and adventures.*

BabyBoomer-Magazine.com

Books to Help You Work for Boomers

Steven Gillon and Nancy Singer Olaguera, *Boomer Nation: The Largest and Richest Generation Ever, and How It Changed America,* **Free Press (May 25, 2004)**
> *This book talks about this powerful generation—they are the decision makers and they are still, after all these years, reshaping America.*

J. Smith Walker, *Generation Ageless: How Baby Boomers Are Changing the Way We Live Today . . . And They're Just Getting Started,* **Collins Business (October 2, 2007)**
> *This is a great resource guide to who and what these people are. If you want to make money from this generation, you need to know what makes them tick—read this book and take notes.*

CHAPTER ELEVEN: The Diverse Face of the Job Market

Okay, we all know boys do have many of the cool jobs, so here's some for the women.

Department of Labor—Women in High-Tech Jobs
> *This Department of Labor site provides information on high-tech jobs available to the "sweeter" gender.*
> DOL.gov

WomensJobList—Jobs for Women; Job Search; Career Advice
> *Search thousands of jobs on the largest job board for women.*
> WomensJobList.com

Association for Women in Science (AWIS)—Careers
> *The "Careers" section of the AWIS Web site (hit the Careers tab on the menu bar) is dedicated to furthering the careers of women in science. They offer, jobs, volunteer work, and internship information.*
> AWIS.org

Women Sports Jobs—Sports Jobs and Sports Career Counseling and Sports Resume for Women

This is a women-in-sports-careers network. This site offers job listings and help with professionally written sports resumes.

WomenSportsJobs.com

MedicalWorkers.com—Women's Health Jobs

MedicalWorkers.com is ideal for finding registered nurse careers and women's health-related jobs.

MedicalWorkers.com

Engineer Girl

Find out more about engineering careers. Read profiles of women engineers. Find out what classes to take in high school to pursue an engineering career.

EngineerGirl.org

Refrigeration School

Far fewer women than men pursue refrigeration and HVAC (heating, ventilating, and air conditioning) certification; heating and cooling certification; or training in electrical technologies. They are also great careers for women.

RefrigerationSchool.com

Contractor School Online—Pass Your State License Exam!

The premiere contractor school to help you pass your state contractor license exam. They offer online trade testing, study materials, and more.

ContractorReferral.com

Ask Patty—Automotive Advice for Women

Patty is a mom, daughter, wife, niece, grandmother, and auntie. Patty is young, old, married, single, an experienced driver, a new driver, a race car driver.

AskPatty.com

National Center for Women and Information Technology (NCWIT)

This site provides military spouse reentry programs helping midcareer women return to work in information technologies (IT).

NCWIT.org

CHAPTER TWELVE: An Endless Summer:
Independents and Freelancers

We shouldn't have to twist your arm to convince you that freelancing and working for yourself is the best of the best. The commute from your bed to the computer is stress free, your boss is only a semijerk, and the perks such as a shower in your office and endless naps are top-notch. So find a job or career path from this list, and good luck! The only downside is if you get fired, you literally only have yourself to blame.

Elance—Connect with Qualified Professionals
Work with freelance Web designers, programmers, SEO firms, XML programmers, and graphic designers who submit proposals for your projects.

Elance.com

Sunoasis—Writing, Journalism, and Copywriter Jobs
Employment opportunities for writers, journalists, and new-media types in reporting and feature writing, reviewing, editing, and freelancing editorial positions.

Sunoasis.com

Writers Digest
Find out about the business of writing.

WritersDigest.com

Poets and Writers (PW)
Contact the nice folks at Poets and Writers to find out about writing competitions, literary magazines, and small presses that welcome both new and established writers. If you're seeking employment in the literary world, be sure to visit their job listings.

PW.org

Writers Write
Find a large directory of information about writing and publishing.

WritersWrite.com

iUniverse—Self-Publish Your Work
Find everything you need to know about self-publishing affordably.

iUniverse.com

Sologig—Freelance Jobs, Contract, and Consulting Projects

Thousands of quality freelance, contract, and consulting projects are posted daily on Sologig.com. Post a resume and apply to top freelance projects easily.

Sologig.com

HotGigs—Consultants: Find Consulting Jobs

Get access to top consulting jobs at this site. Also, promote your consultant profile to HotGigs' network of experts.

HotGigs.com

iFreelance—Freelance Animators

Find freelance animators; browse the database of freelance animators or post your projects.

iFreelance.com

Tech_centric—Computer, Tech, and IT Jobs Search

Search computer jobs, tech jobs, IT jobs, IT employment postings, and hot IT careers at Tech-Centric.net. Post your resume.

Tech-centric.net

Nolo—Consulting and Contracting, Resource Center

Get the forms and information that independent contractors need. Create solid contracts, get paid on time, and deal with the IRS successfully.

Nolo.com

FreelanceSwitch—Freelance Advice and Freelance Jobs

This popular blog gives you advice on becoming a freelancer.

FreelanceSwitch.com

Volunteer Solutions—Learn to Tutor Adults

If you have ever considered tutoring an adult to read or speak English but thought you wouldn't know where to begin, here is a chance to learn how.

Volunteer.united-e-way.org

National Association for Fitness Certification (NAFC)— Personal Trainer Certification, Fitness Certification

NAFCtrainer.com

Body Basics
Do you want to learn how to be the best personal trainer, fitness instructor, aerobics instructor, or wellness consultant possible? Here's a site for you.

Body-Basics.com

New York Life—Becoming an Insurance Sales Agent
Learn to sell insurance and make money as an independent contractor.

NewYorkLife.com

Coto Insurance and Financial Services—Becoming an Insurance Sales Agent
Coto Insurance and Financial Services offers the ambitious individual an opportunity to earn substantial income, and be just like Vicki Gunvalson, the Orange County homemaker who runs this successful company.

CotoInsurance.com

CHAPTER THIRTEEN: Treading Water in Creative Industries: The Art of Selling Art

Lucky for you—there's help for creative people, and you won't have to starve because there's no way to get your opus out there.

Artists House Music
Helping musicians and entrepreneurs create sustainable careers. For both novices and professionals, here's some practical guidance on performing in bars, clubs, and theaters. This site provides a guide to recording sessions, composing for TV and radio advertisements for instrumentalists, composers, arrangers, and producers.

ArtistsHouseMusic.org

Digital Musician
Learn how to make money as a digital musician with computers and the Internet.

DigitalMusician.net

Musicouch
This site provides practical tips on how to earn an income playing a musical instrument.

Musicouch.com

Springboard for the Arts
This organization is committed to helping artists make a living, get career counseling, and training.

SpringBoardForTheArts.org

Juried Online Arts Festival (JOLAF)
This is a contemporary online arts and crafts gallery where collectors buy and artists sell their works.

JOLAF.com

Mid Atlantic Arts Foundation (MAAF)
Find help and support for artists and art organizations in the mid Atlantic and beyond. Find out about grants, news, events, and resources.

MidAtlanticArts.org

Art Deadlines List
Find art contests and competitions, art jobs and internships, art scholarships, grants, and fellowships, art festivals, calls for entries/ proposals/projects, and other opportunities, in all disciplines, for art students, art teachers, and artists of all ages.

ArtDeadlinesList.com

Demand Studios—Get Hired to Write for Web sites
There are jobs aplenty for writers, editors, copyeditors, and filmmakers.

DemandStudios.com

Guru—Directory for Freelancers
This is an online service marketplace for freelancers. Register and advertise your creative service as a freelancer, and use this site to build your clientele. It is great for writers, artists, Web and product designers, and many others.

Guru.com

Media Match
This is a job listing guide to find production jobs or production crews. Find useful resources for TV and the film industry.

Media-Match.com

Actingbiz.com—Online Actors Resource

The site provides help for actors to launch a career, find auditions, work as an extra, and more.

ActingBiz.com

My Acting Site

This is a Web site source for actors, voiceover talent, and models, with provision for your own domain name, resume page, and photo gallery. You can build your Web site here and access the Actor's Resource Center with information and tips on how to book work with the casting directors of Hollywood.

MyActingSite.com

Judy Carter's Comedy Workshops

Want to be a comedian? Find out how to start and enjoy a career as a standup comic.

ComedyWorkshops.com

Chuckle Monkey

Comedians can get listed here and find out about comedy clubs, gigs, and booking agents.

ChuckleMonkey.com

Film Staff

This is your source for gigs in the entertainment business. Film production and television production listings are updated daily, as well as jobs on commercials, music videos, theater, and interactive projects.

FilmStaff.com

Resource Book on Publicity for Musicians and Bands

Find out how to garner publicity for your band:

Randy Chertkow and Jason Feehan, *The Indie Band Survival Guide: The Complete Manual for the Do-It-Yourself Musician*, St. Martin's Griffin (August 5, 2008)

For all you "Spinal Tap" wannabes, this book turns metal-heads into techno-geeks. The authors cover topics such as networking, branding, creating a Web site, getting booked, playing live, and getting publicized, because if you want to make money, it's not just about the music.

CHAPTER FOURTEEN: Filling the Money Pipeline: Internet Marketing Options

Rush hour traffic is so yesterday! Time clocks? Paychecks every other week? These will soon be mere artifacts of the life you left behind to become an Internet mogul.

Great Internet Marketing—Internet Marketing Training
This site gives you everything you need to know about creating products and marketing them online.
> GreatInternetMarketing.com

Pro Marketing Online—Marketing Tools Guide
Find out about the latest tools for monetizing your Web site.
> Pro-Marketing-Online.com

Marketing Tool Guide—Concise, Impartial, and Easy to Use
Find a weekly review/report of the latest Internet marketing tools.
> MarketingToolGuide.com

cdzn.com—The Best Internet Marketing Tools
Find Internet expert, Michael Campbell's favorite eBooks, courses, tools, and software. Here you can find tips, tricks, and strategies. Use them to do keyword research, find niches, examine your competitors, enhance your search engine positioning, and get the most out of your paid advertising.
> cdzn.com

Affiliate Helper—How to Earn Money with Affiliates
Check out the latest reviews of affiliate and Internet marketing tools.
> AffHelper.com

Startup Internet Marketing
Find a weekly review/report of the latest Internet marketing tools.
> StartupInternetMarketing.com

Marketing Scoop—Internet Marketing Expert Resources
Check out resources in major marketing disciplines that include advertising, direct marketing, Internet marketing, search engine optimization, market research, strategy, public relations, and trade shows.
> MarketingScoop.com

Iterating—A Wiki-Based Software Guide
This is a huge compilation of Wiki-based Internet marketing software guides, user reviews, and more.

Iterating.com

SubHub—Build Your Own Revenue-Ready Web Site
SubHub is an online publishing platform that makes it easy for you to build your own content Web site. Make money from subscription/ membership, advertising, affiliate marketing, or selling stuff via a store.

SubHub.com

CHAPTER FIFTEEN: Ride the Worldwide Wave: Go Global

Tired of pounding the same old pavement for work? If you're searching all over and going nowhere, maybe its time to get out of here and find a job in another country. You only live once, but a change of scenery might feel like you're getting another life. Try it. What's the worst that could happen? That you'll fall in love and never come back?

How to Connect with Overseas Recruiters and Job Placement Agencies

Teleport My Job—Where Do You Want to Be?
Are you a professional trying to figure out how to relocate your career to some of the fastest growing and most exciting cities in the world? Start exploring here.

TeleportMyJob.com

JobServe—Daily Up-to-the-Minute Opportunities
JobServe currently operates in 17 industry sectors and advertises jobs from all over the world. They advertise over 2.5 million jobs a year. "Jobs by e-mail" is sent immediately via e-mail, SMS, RSS, and even by phone hotline if you call for details.

JobServe.com

Getting Yourself Situated in a Foreign Country

Escape Artist—Living Overseas, Jobs, Real Estate, and Asset Protection

This online magazine and index of international employment resources has an eye-popping assortment of articles on exotic and unique ways of living overseas. Want to live on a barge in Europe? How about a yachting career? Can you form your own micro nation? Learn how here.

EscapeArtist.com

Shelter Offshore—Live, Work, and Buy Property Abroad

Shelter Offshore serves expatriates around the world, providing services, information, and resources to help make moving or living abroad easier.

ShelterOffshore.com

Overseas Digest—The Adventure of Living and Working Abroad

This is an expatriate's guide to living and working overseas. Everything you need to know about jobs, teaching, healthcare, moving, money, and taxes.

OverseasDigest.com

Working for Nonprofits, Internships, and Volunteer Projects

Idealist—The Resource Guide for International Careers in Nonprofit Programs

Idealist is an interactive site where people and organizations can exchange resources and ideas, locate opportunities, and supporters.

Idealist.org

Humanitarian Relief

Having trouble getting your foot in the door? It's easier by volunteering or through an internship.

HumanitarianRelief.change.org

Earn a Living Teaching English in Other Countries

Council on International Educational Exchange (CIEE)
Whether you are a recent graduate, an experienced teacher, or a professional ready for a change, CIEE is devoted to increasing opportunities for you to teach abroad.

CIEE.org

Interac—Japan's Leading Private Provider of Assistant Language Teachers
Help teach English in Japan—guaranteed pay, bonuses, benefits, and holidays. Do you like sushi?

Interac.co.jp

English First—Online Recruitment Center for Teaching Overseas
Find jobs for teaching English all over the world, and how to get started.

EnglishFirst.com

So You've Always Wanted to Be a Canadian?

Canada Visa
This site includes ways to work, live, and immigrate to Canada

CanadaVisa.com

Jobs in Canada
This site is easy to use, and there is a plethora of jobs to be found all across the Great White North.

JobsInCanada.com

Get Paid to Tour the World

International Tour Management Institute (ITMI)—Training Programs
Get certified to operate tours all over the world. Train to become a professional tour director.

ITMITourTraining.com

Notes

Chapter One:

page 8, "...you're catapulted into another adventure": Liz Smith, "Women for Hire Presents Wildly Wise, Witty and Wondrous Voices," WomenForHire.com, www.womenforhire.com/be_gutsy/audio_inspiration, December 8, 2008.

Chapter Two:

page 24:, ... 35 percent of Americans were very happy: Harissinteractive .com, www.harrisinteractive.com/harris_poll/pubs/Harris_Poll_2009_05_15.pdf, May 15, 2009.

Chapter Four:

page 37, ... it is a breakthrough: Landmark Education, www.landmarkeducation.com/landmark_forum_educational_methodology .jsp.

page 43, "... doesn't require a college degree," he said: Susan Todd, "Coffee Break: Rutgers Professor Talks About National Skills Strategy in Tough Job Market," *The Star-Ledger*, www.nj.com/business/index .ssf/2009/05/coffee_break_rutgers_professor.html, May 13, 2009.

Chapter Eight:

page 73, "... reduce waste and pollution and benefit the environment": http://apolloalliance.org.

page 73, "... help solve our environmental problems": www.greenforall.org/about-us/our-mission.

page 74, "... bigger than the Internet": Gerard Wynn, "Clean Technology Bigger than Internet-Software Guru," Reuters, www.alertnet.org/thenews/newsdesk/L15635392.htm, May 15, 2007.

page 75, ... $66 billion in 2007: "Innovations for a Sustainable Economy State of the World," Worldwatch.org, 2008.

page 76, ... renewable energy and energy-efficiency industries: Alasdair Cameron, "Working with the Wind: Growing Employment in the European and U.S. Wind Power Sectors," *Renewable Energy Magazine*, www.renewableenergyworld.com/rea/news/article/2009/04/working-with-the-wind-growing-employment-in-the-european-and-us-wind-power-sectors, April 2, 2009.

page 77, ... faces a looming labor shortage: Policyarchive.org, hdl.handle .net/10207/7712, 2008.

page 80, ... commissioned by the American Solar Energy Society: Douglas MacMillan, "Switching to Green Collar Jobs," *BusinessWeek*, www.businessweek.com/managing/content/jan2008/ca2008018_005632.htm, January 10, 2008.

page 80, ... Jones wrote in his book, The Green Collar Economy: Van Jones, *The Green Collar Economy*, HarperCollins, 2008, p. 9.

page 81, ... spearheaded the Clean Energy Jobs Bill: Thomas Friedman, "The Green Collar Solution," *The New York Times*, www.nytimes .com/2007/10/17/opinion/17friedman.html, October 17, 2007.

page 81, ... commit $1 billion a year to energy efficiency: IBM press room, 03.ibm.com/press/us/, May 2007.

page 84, ... like machinists and technicians: Joe Loughrey, "Manufacturing a Better Future for our Young People," National Association of Manufacturers, www.nam.org/NewsFromtheNAM/Press%20 Releases/MI/Manufacturingabetterfutureforouryoungpeople.aspx (originally published in *The Buffalo News*, June 4, 2006).

page 86, ... released by the Pew Charitable Trusts: Brandon MacGillis and Andrew McDonald, "Pew Finds Clean Energy Economy Generates Significant Job Growth," *The Pew Charitable Trusts*, Pewtrusts.org/ news_room, June 10, 2009.

Chapter Nine:

page 92, ... 50 best Web sites of 2008: Anita Hamilton "50 Best Websites," *Time*, Time.com/time/specials/2007/article/, 2007.

page 93, Top Industries Aimed at Making a Profit from Generation Y: Independent Thank You for Firing Me! Poll, 500 participants, January 2009–May 2009.

page 97, ... a survey in 2008 by Robert Half International: Andrew Tilin, "Recruiting Gen Y: Four Killer Tactics," *BNET*, www.bnet .com/2403-13059_23-201796.html, May 20, 2008.

page 98, ... according to the U.S. Bureau of the Census: U.S. Census Bureau, "Educational Attainment," Census.gov/population/www/socdemo/ educ-attn.html, 2008.

page 101, ... is available to more than six billion people worldwide: "The Internet Big Picture," Internet World Stats, http://Internetworldstats .com/stats.htm, March 31, 2009.

page 102, ... 10.5 hours of TV a week: Marc Battaglia, "Millenials (18-24 Year Olds) Watch Less TV, More Streaming Video but Respond to Physical Media," Demi & Cooper Advertising, "Charles Chat," http://demicooper.com/blog/2008/12/26/, December 26, 2008.

page 104, ... released by Xola Consulting, Inc.: "Beyond the Adrenaline Rush: Rethinking Traditional Adventure Travel Marketing for Gen Y," *Adventure Travel News*, http://www.adventuretravelnews.com/ beyond-the-adrenaline-rush-rethinking-traditional-adventure-travel-marketing-for-gen-y, August 22, 2008.

page 105, ... according to USA Today: Barbara Katz, "Focus on Generation Y," *Health Focus International*, August 22, 2007.

page 106, ... Wharf Research Division of the Center for Culinary Development: Marc Halperin, "Crunch Time" *QSR Magazine*, www.qsrmagazine .com/articles/menu_development/117/snacks-1.phtml, July 2008.

page 107, ... 83 percent of purchases: *Wine & Spirits Daily*, winespiritsdaily .com, May 21, 2008.

Chapter Ten:

page 109, ... total net worth of American households: Dean Burns, "The Influence of the Baby Boomer Generation," *Baby Boomer Magazine*, www.babyboomer-magazine.com/news/165/ ARTICLE/1207/2009-05-22.html, May 22, 2009.

page 110, ... Harris Interactive and Principal Financial Group online survey: Principal.com/about/news, December 3, 2008.

page 110, "... already facing job shortages": Mark Freedman, *Public Affairs*, August 25, 2008, p. 23.

page 111, ... put out in 2008 by the Urban Institute: Richard W. Johnson, "How Is the Recession Affecting Older Workers?" The Urban Institute, www.urban.org/UploadedPDF/411804_recession_affects .pdf, December 2008.

page 116, ... *annual income of more than $40 million*: Nicholas K. Geranios, "Jimmy Buffett Sells the Idea of Good Times," *Chicago Tribune*, http://archives.chicagotribune.com/2009/jan/06/travel/chi-buffett-empire-0106jan06, January 6, 2009.

page 118, ... *joint study by TNS Compete and the Consumer Electronics Association*: "Frustrations with Technology Provide an Opportunity for Companies to Better Address the Needs of Older Americans," Competeinc.com, www.competeinc.com/news_events/ pressReleases/221/, January 7, 2009.

page 118, ... *"Greying Gadgets: How Older Americans Shop for and Use Consumer Electronics"*: Consumer Electronics Association, Market Research.com, Marketresearch.com/product/display, March 31, 2009.

page 119, ... *if they want to strike gold*: Christopher Musico, "The Boomer Boom," Destination CRM.com, /www.destinationcrm.com/Articles/ Editorial/Magazine-Features/The-Boomer-Boom-51407.aspx, November 1, 2008.

page 120, *"A company called Travel Marketing Decisions ..."*: Kim Ross, "13 Truths About Baby Boomer Travel," *Travel Marketing Decisions*, www.atme.org/pubs/archives/77_253_1108.cfm [N.D.].

page 120, ... up from 62 percent one year ago: TravelDailyNews.com, October 2, 2008.

page 121, ... *polled in a Travel Industry Association survey*: TravelDailyNews .com, December 30, 2008.

page 121, ... *by the Specialty Travel Agents Association*: Specialtytravelagents .com.

page 122, ... *according to Kaiser Foundation*: Susan Donaldson James, "Baby Boomers Fuel Thriving Health Industry," ABC News, http://abcnews .go.com/Business/story?id=5389800&page=1, July 17, 2008.

page 122, ... a report from the Bureau of Labor Statistics: Bureau of Labor Statistics, Bls.gov/oco.

page 122, ... 39,500 assisted living facilities: Chip Zimmer, "The Boomers Are Coming! The Boomers Are Coming!" *McKnight's Long-Term Care News & Assisted Living*, Mcknights.com, January 13, 2009.

page 123, A franchise with BrightStar ...: FindAFranchise.com.

page 123, ... to exceed $2 billion by 2015: Sheryl Ubelacker, "Popularity of Brain-Fitness Games Soaring, but Do They Really Work?" *The Canadian Press*, April 7, 2009.

page 123, ... will have Alzheimer's by 2050: John Hopkins University, Department of Biostatistics Working Papers, paper 130, 2007; Ron Brookmeyer, Elizabeth Johnson, Kathryn Ziegler-Graham, and H. Michael Arrgihi, "Forecasting the Global Burden of Alzheimer's Disease," 2008bepress.com.

page 125, ... a survey conducted by AARP: Jeff Jenkins, "Luxury Rentals: A New Option for Active Adult Living," *Nation's Building News Online*, Chapter 11: www.nbnnews.com/NBN/textonly/2005-11-07/printall .html, November 7, 2005.

Chapter Eleven:

page 126 , ... generated nearly $2 trillion in sales: "Women Own More than 10 Million Businesses," Lahle Wolfe, *About.com Guide to Women in Business*, http://WomenInBusiness.About.com/b/2009/08/04/ women-own-more-than-10-million-businesses.htm, August 4, 2009.

page 129, ... 2006 Federal Aviation Administration Airman data: www.faa.gov/data_research/aviation_data_statistics/civil_airmen_ statistics/2006/.

page 130, ... studies compiled by Catalyst: Research and Knowledge, Catalyst.org.

page 135, ... on a report card: Engineers Make the Case for 2009 Report Card's D Grade, ASCE.org.

page 135, ... $2 billion annually on repairs and maintenance: National Fact Sheet, Asce.org/reportcard.

page 135, ... under the supervision of the Department of Labor: Mark Silva, "Obama's Summer Jobs Plan: Work for 600,000 People," *Los Angeles Times*, www.latimes.com/news/nationworld/nation/la-na-obama-jobs9-2009jun09,0,4293370.story, June 8, 2009.

Chapter Fourteen:

page 166, ... generates $10 million per year: Max Chafkin, "And the Money Comes Rolling In," *Inc.*, January/February 2009, pp. 62–69.

page 169, ... according to a report in Fast Company *magazine:* Chuck Salter, "Girl Power," *Fast Company*, September Issue 119, fastcompany. com/118/girl.power, 2007.

page 173, ... display on their home page: Sam Zuckerman, "Yes, Some Blogs Are Profitable—Very Profitable," *San Francisco Chronicle*, www.sfgate.com/cgi-bin/article.cgi?file=/c/a/2007/10/21/BUVJSNSTC.DTL, October 21, 2007

Chapter Fifteen:

page 178, ... Manpower, Inc.'s 2009 Talent Shortage survey: Barton Eckert, "Manpower; Employers Struggling to Find Qualified Job Candidates," *Washington Business Journal*, www.bizjournals.com/tampabay/stories/2009/05/25/daily52.html, May 28, 2009.

Conclusion:

page 185, ... the highest since 1974: David Goldman, "Lost: 1.9 Million Jobs," *CNNMoney.com*, http://money.cnn.com/2008/12/05/news/economy/jobs_november/index.htm, December 5, 2008.

page 187, ... *began in December 2007:* Shobhana Chandra, "U.S. Initial Jobless Claims Decreased Last Week," *Bloomberg Press*, www.bloomberg.com/apps/news, June 11, 2009.

Index of Companies and Web Sites

Note: Page numbers in *italics* indicate references to the Resource Guide.

General Index